drop

Making Great Decisions

USE **NEUROSCIENCE** TO RETRAIN
YOUR BRAIN AND
MAKE BETTER LIFE CHOICES

Dr. Helen McKibben

Copyright © 2024 by Dr. Helen McKibben

Published in the United States by Feelings Management Press, an imprint of Feelings Management LLC, Bethesda, Maryland. First edition 2024

Cover design by Emily Mahon.
Cover photo by Didssph on Unsplash.
Interior design by Rebecca Brown.

All rights reserved. No portion of this book may be reproduced, distributed, or transmitted in any form or by any means without the prior written permission from the publisher or author, except as permitted by U.S. copyright law. For permission requests, please contact Dr. Helen McKibben at contact@HelenMcKibben.com.

ISBN: 979-8-9863889-0-8 (Paperback)
ISBN: 979-8-9863889-1-5 (eBook)
ISBN: 979-8-9863889-2-2 (Audiobook)

Library of Congress Control Number: 2023922080

Important Note: Limitation of Liability and Disclaimer of Warranty: This book is not intended as a substitute for the medical or clinical recommendation of healthcare providers; rather, it is intended to offer information to help the reader cooperate with health professionals in a mutual quest for optimum well-being. The advice and strategies contained herein may not be suitable for your situation. You should consult with a professional prior to using any of the information in this book.

While the publisher and author have used their best efforts in preparing this book, they make no representations or warranties with respect to the accuracy or completeness of its contents and specifically disclaim any implied warranties of merchantability or fitness for a particular purpose. Neither the publisher nor the author shall be liable for any loss of profit or any other commercial damages, including but not limited to special, incidental, consequential, personal, or other damages.

The identities of the interview subjects and any references to people and places described in the interviews have been changed to protect their confidentiality. All interview subjects were volunteers who agreed to appear in the book. None of the interview subjects currently are or have ever been clients of the author as part of the author's private counseling practice.

FEELINGS MANAGEMENT® is a registered trademark of Feelings Management LLC. Use of the trademark without express permission is prohibited.

www.HelenMcKibben.com

Contents

Preface

Introduction:
How to Drop to the Blank Screen 6

Chapter 1
Rewiring Your Brain 12

Chapter 2
Redefining Self-Esteem 23

Chapter 3
Overcoming the Critical Voice 31

Chapter 4
Substance Abuse and Managing the
Addictive Voice 48

Chapter 5
Disordered Eating and How the
Brain Guides What We Eat 62

Chapter 6
Getting Sleep and Using Your
Dreams to Resolve Feelings 81

Chapter 7
   External Disruptors: Dealing with
   Difficult People..*91*

Chapter 8
   Parenting: Influencing Your Child's
   Self-Esteem *118*

Chapter 9
   Dating in Neutral: How to Change
   Who You Attract *142*

Chapter 10
   Emotional Muscle: How Athletes
   and Performers Succeed.......................*178*

Chapter 11
   Trusting Your Brain: It's Scientific.....*203*

Acknowledgements

Dedications

This book is dedicated to people in my past, present, and future. In the past, I dedicate this book to my father and Greg for supporting and promoting my self-esteem. In the present, I thank my colleagues for giving me the clinical setting to practice my methodology. In the future, the dedication goes to my sons, John and Jacob, who will transfer these acquired skills to their future interactions.

Preface

Our society is suffering from the effects of a "feeling disease" that results in procrastination, lack of follow-through, ineffective relationships, and costly disabilities such as anxiety, depression, and substance abuse. So far, the response of the self-help industry to this national crisis has largely been to teach us how to override our feelings. Book after book and podcast after podcast guide readers through methods of breathing, relaxation, or meditation to help them clear their minds of negative emotions. However, methods of relaxation are often temporary Band-Aids to addressing stress and emotional reactions. If people do not allow themselves to explore their triggered feelings, that relief will not be permanent. Tensions and stress will remain, continuing to build in the body and being retriggered over and over again, until the enormous volume of ignored or "bottled-up" emotions becomes overwhelming.

The problem with traditional self-help techniques is that they rob us of the very things we need to make good decisions for ourselves: the words that accompany our feelings. I believe that, in order to make healthy decisions, we must learn to stop running from our emotions. Instead, we must learn to feel first and think second, no longer running from our emotions. The brain just works better that way.

With this in mind, during my thirty-five years of experience as a clinical therapist, I have totally redefined the concept of *self-esteem*. Far from encouraging my clients to relax and clear their minds, I teach individuals to do the opposite: To feel through their emotions and listen to themselves long enough to hear what they need to do for themselves—then to take well-considered action based on their real needs. My revolutionary approach taps into the biomechanics of emotion, based on the premise that people and situations trigger emotions, and the first receptors for those emotions are physical, not cognitive. If people who struggle to make healthy decisions for themselves (physically, cognitively, and emotionally) focus only on their thoughts and don't deal with this physiology (that is, with the changes in physical and chemical processes occurring in the body, which I will often refer to the physical aspects of), they will continue to overreact, sabotaging their progress through life. On the contrary, permanent, neuromuscular relief comes when people allow themselves to feel before they think, completing the entire sequence of working through their feelings and, only then, making decisions when the brain is functioning at optimum levels.

> Permanent, neuromuscular relief comes when people allow themselves to feel before they think.

That is what *Drop: Making Great Decisions* is all about.

The method is called *dropping to the blank screen* (*dropping* or *drop* for short), and you'll learn more about how it works in the Introduction. But first, let me take a moment to give you an overview of the book you hold in your hands.

This book is intended as a companion piece to the extended *Drop: Making Great Decisions* audiobook, and it is designed to be more than just a self-help book. While other self-help books suggest ways of being in order to live a better life, mine goes a step further, offering a tried-and-true method for *attaining* that optimum lifestyle through enhanced decision-making.

The instructions in this book will help people identify indicators of poor self-listening skills, enable them to make those indicators conscious, and teach them how to rewire their brains to change their responses to life's stressors. Throughout, I've included transcripts of conversations with interview subjects (under pseudonyms) who consented to appear in this book. These conversations have been edited for length and clarity, with the purpose of illustrating how real people have applied the *drop* method to various aspects of their lives.

I encourage you to read this book—and listen to the expanded audiobook—from beginning to end. However, you may also jump around to individual topics, as the underlying methodology is the same for each, in order to find value in the material that's most applicable to your life. Please note that, if you do decide to dip in and out based on the topics that call to you, you'll need to read the Introduction and chapters 1 through 3 first to get the foundational material you need to follow the real-world advice provided in chapters 4 through 11 for applying my methodology to your life.

By practicing the *drop* method, you will learn a myriad of new skills. They include learning to stop second-guessing yourself, to stop worrying and predicting, and to stop reacting to others. You'll stop being distracted, attracting difficult personalities and unprofessional relationships, procrastinating, and learn to follow through with your ideas. You'll also gain the power to break any dependencies on drugs and alcohol, and even to enhance physical performance. This book teaches how to embody self-esteem in a deeper way than the clichéd "I like myself." In summary, you will learn to identify and use untapped emotional instincts to make decisions in accordance with your specific concerns and needs.

> You will learn to identify and use untapped emotional instincts to make decisions in accordance with your specific concerns and needs.

Introduction:
How to Drop to the Blank Screen

The cornerstone of my methodology is a technique I call *dropping to the blank screen*. If you practice this technique every time you experience a *triggered feeling*—an emotion such as anger, sadness, or confusion that causes a physiological and psychological reaction—you will benefit from the memory-retrieval processes involved in smart decision-making.

What do I mean by that?

People who make decisions through thinking alone, by trying to think through the perfect thing to do, are actually running away from the very feelings and memories that could help them make good decisions. If, as you begin to experience a triggered feeling, you *drop to the blank screen*, you give your brain an opportunity to remember every time you felt that way before and incorporate those memories into your current decision-making. This approach will resolve the triggered feeling and prevent you from retriggering that same feeling again later.

So, what is the *blank screen*, and how do we *drop* there?

The first thing I'm going to teach you is the physical position you need to be in to *drop to the blank screen*. Practice this position so that whenever you experience a triggered feeling that's threatening to overwhelm you, you can take yourself physically to this position to work through it.

Sit in a chair with a back on it and feel the full weight of your lower body being totally supported by the surface beneath you. Be sure your hips aren't locked. They should be released enough to feel the full weight of the legs. You're totally supported, like dead weight on the chair, with no readiness—and no inclination—to get up and move.

Likewise, your upper body weight is fully supported by the surface behind you. Your shoulders aren't scrunched up beside your ears or pulling into their sockets, but released enough to feel the full, dead weight of your arms against the chair.

Your tongue isn't pushing against the roof of your mouth or the front of your teeth. And your throat is open enough to feel air go down into your lungs.

This neutral position you're now in is the *blank screen.*

Your breathing and heart rate are even, your muscles are elongated, and thoughts are not spinning in your head. In this position, your brain receives maximum oxygen and blood flow and operates very efficiently in making decisions. Reaching this *blank screen* position indicates that you have not been triggered to feel yet. Or, if you were triggered to feel recently, you have made it through the feeling, and now sit in readiness to listen to yourself and make good decisions.

Why is that important?

Because if we don't allow ourselves to go through feelings that trigger us, we can't be effective decision-makers. When we *drop to the blank screen*, one of the most important things that happens is that the brain and the body return to neutral. *Dropping* resolves the physiological responses to each triggered feeling (that is, with the changes in physical and chemical processes occurring in the body, which I will often refer to the physical aspects of). I'll discuss the science of *dropping* in more detail in Chapter 11.

> When we drop to the blank screen, one of the most important things that happens is that the brain and the body return to neutral.

The other important thing that this technique does is activate the brain. The brain is designed to spend just nanoseconds recalling and configuring every memory of the times you've felt a particular dilemma or trigger before. If you let it, your brain will show you what's worked for you and what hasn't in similar past experiences. It configures all those facts and details so clearly that you will actually hear your brain spit out simple words or ideas about what you could do to find permanent, healthy relief from your triggered feeling.

Once you've *dropped*, keep focusing on feeling the full weight of your legs, the full weight of your arms, and the air going down into your lungs. Sit with that until you start to hear the simple words or ideas that empower you to make decisions as opposed to reacting. Once you've made the decision about what to say or do, you'll feel the triggered feeling resolve completely, and the brain won't have to keep bringing up the memory or the thoughts over and over again.

Why is this important?

Because if a feeling isn't fully felt through and resolved by making an intentional decision, the brain is designed to keep bringing the feeling up until it is. This is problematic because, with each of those thoughts, feelings, or memories, a physiological and/or physical reaction occurs: increased heart rate, higher blood pressure, nervous laughter, holding your breath, or tense muscles. I call this *lighting up*—experiencing bodily changes from feeling something uncomfortable. And as those reactions continue to build one thought or one feeling at a time, they can lead to anxiety, depression, sleeplessness, chronic pain—you name it. But when you make the important shift of noticing where you're *lighting up*, then *dropping* until you're back at the blank screen, you activate your brain in the way it's designed to work and give yourself space to truly resolve the physiological response rather than just shoving it away to deal with later.

I offer you three warnings about pitfalls you might encounter while experimenting with the technique of *dropping to the blank screen*. The good news is, each pitfall can be overcome with practice and perseverance.

You might add this technique to your repertoire for a few days, and then find yourself reverting to old techniques of running from feelings. Keep intentionally *dropping* until it becomes your default approach.

It can take several *drops* to get to the *blank screen*. When you are triggered, if unresolved past feelings resurface, you'll have to *drop* through all of those old feelings to get to the *blank screen*. Take the time to *drop* through all those old feelings.

When using the technique to deal with other people who trigger you, they may become more agitated and try to disrupt you even more. Stand your ground.

By learning to overcome those pitfalls and make *dropping to the blank screen* your go-to method for dealing with triggered feelings, you will give yourself a unique and powerful tool. As we move through the book, we'll look at a variety of ways to put this technique into practice, but before we do that, let's recap the three key things *dropping* simultaneously achieves: First, *dropping* resolves the physiological response that is activated with every single triggered feeling and returns the body to a neutral physiological stance. Second, this method activates the brain to retrieve memories of every time the practitioner has felt this way before. Third, *dropping* allows you to listen to your own thoughts, feelings, and ideas to help make excellent decisions. We call that high self-esteem.

Chapter 1
Rewiring Your Brain

Before you can begin effectively using this methodology of *dropping to the blank screen*, I will give you some homework to help your brain add a new configuration to its old neuron tracks, training it to support you in the constructive decision-making process I've just described. I've broken your homework into four "assignments" that will teach you how to use *dropping to the blank screen* with your stressors.

Assignment One:
Observing Your Critical Voice

The critical voice is a continuous inner dialogue that surfaces and tries to make you second-guess whatever you've just said or done.

"Why'd you do this?"

"You should have done that instead."

"They think this about you."

"That won't work."

Some people's critical voices are very loud, while others' are weaker or may not exist at all. Your first assignment is to find out if you have one or not. Over the next twenty-four-hour period, count how many times you find yourself up in your head, listening to a dialogue that makes you second-guess yourself, criticizes you, or tells you what to do.

Assignment Two:
Identifying How You Manage Triggered Feelings

Feelings are triggered all day long. They're triggered by people, they're triggered by situations, and they're even triggered just by *thinking* about people and situations. What we want to find out in this second homework assignment is whether your current style of managing triggered feelings is effective. If not, you'll want to add *dropping to the blank screen* to your repertoire.

There are three styles of managing feelings.

Running from Feelings

In this Number One style, an individual gets triggered by a person, situation, or thought and immediately gets busy thinking of the perfect strategy to respond. And while they're all up in their head, they rearrange their bedroom, they jog ten miles, they call somebody on the phone, and then they come back and rearrange the living room or the kitchen, too. This individual habitually runs from feelings by keeping cognitively or physically busy, including worrying, predicting the future, thinking about past experiences, or doing anything else to not feel. The result is that the individual never goes through the feelings that are getting triggered. They run from them.

Within this Number One style of managing feelings is a variant called "painting pictures," where someone goes up in their head and starts predicting outcomes before they've even happened.

"It's going to turn out this way."

"Well, if I do this, they'll do that."

Painting pictures is a detrimental style of managing feelings, because when the individual has painted a picture of what's *going* to happen, they're likely to be devastated when it doesn't happen exactly the way they thought it would.

Sitting on Feelings

With style Number Two, a person who has been triggered simply sits on the feeling by dismissing or minimizing their emotion psychically and cognitively.

"Oh, I'm fine."

"No, I'm good."

"What did you want me to do?"

"Sure, put that on my desk. I'll get the work done for you. No problem."

Every time they're triggered to feel, they deny or push away the feeling until one of two things eventually happens: Those avoided feelings build until the individual either explodes into provocation, anxiety, or panic; or those avoided feelings cause the individual to implode into depression.

Making Decisions

The Number Three style of managing feelings is when the individual, once triggered to feel, notices something's up and responds immediately by sitting back with themselves long enough to hear their own words and point of view. When they're ready, they make decisions, never second-guessing how they feel or what they've just heard in themselves.

You can probably tell which strategies are ineffective and which one is healthy. If you identify as someone who runs from your feelings or sits on them, then it's time to make a change, and this book will help you do it.

What current style do you use in managing feelings? Take the time to observe yourself and how you manage your feelings.

Assignment Three: Recognizing Disruptors

The third homework assignment is about recognizing the people who jar you out of your neutral, *blank screen* perspective. Imagine that you're going through your day, and everything is fine. Then someone calls you, approaches you for a conversation, emails you, or texts you. By the time the interaction is over, you have gone from feeling fine to experiencing a triggered feeling. You can't stop thinking about the disruption.

Your homework is to go out and observe who in your life is disruptive when they approach. Once you've identified the people most likely to trigger feelings in your everyday life, my job is to teach you how to reverse that and go on with your day.

Assignment Four:
Understanding Your Physical Response to Emotions

In the fourth homework assignment, you will learn to identify the onset of a triggered feeling as soon as possible so you can resolve it. When you are triggered to feel, the brain's first response is not cognitive or informative. Your brain doesn't speak up and say, "Oh, you're angry. You should do this." By the time cognition kicks in, feelings have already built up to imposing volumes.

Rather than letting that happen, identify the onset of a feeling as quickly as possible to resolve it. When you are triggered to feel, your brain's first response is to light you up physically: rolling your eyes, walking out of a room, having an increased heart rate, holding your breath, or tightening your muscles. A physical and biochemical reaction accompanies every triggered feeling, but the nature of that reaction is unique to you.

How do you find out where you feel your feelings?

Start by attaching the fourth homework assignment to the first three homework assignments. So when you realize *Oh, that's the fifth time today I've listened to the critical voice,* shift focus and notice what you are feeling physically. When you catch yourself running from or sitting with your feelings, also notice where you're lighting up physically.

When someone texts you and says, "You wouldn't believe what the boss said about you," and you find yourself up all night thinking about it, notice where you feel the feeling.

Once you've noticed where you're feeling the feeling, then you can *drop to the blank screen,* go through it, and respond. This is the quickest method to identify and resolve a triggered feeling.

Now that you've completed all four homework assignments, let's do a practice exercise. I'll be disruptive, and you note where you respond physically, then *drop to the blank screen* and decide how to respond based on the first words you hear in yourself.

For teaching purposes, please start by sitting back in your *blank screen*. Notice that your lower body weight is supported by the surface beneath you, that your hips are released instead of locked, and that you can feel the full weight of your legs, totally supported by the chair and the floor beneath your feet.

Your upper body weight is supported by the surface behind you. Your shoulders are released enough to feel the full dead weight of your arms. Your tongue isn't pushing against the roof of your mouth or the front of your teeth, and your throat is open enough to feel the air going down into your lungs. You're in the *blank screen*, not yet triggered to feel.

In a moment I am going to make **two statements**, and the very first thing I want you to do is observe if they take you out of this *blank screen*. Notice the first areas that are "lighting up" or physically activated, and then *drop back to the blank screen* until that lit-up area returns to neutral.

Please begin to *drop* by feeling the weight of your legs, the weight of your arms, and the air going down into your lungs.

> "I think neuroscience is a hoax."
> "The brain is not designed to work emotionally."

Notice each unique area of your body that's possibly lighting up right now: furrowed brow, rolling eyes, pounding heart, tensing muscles.

Now, *drop* your entire body weight until you're completely back to the *blank screen* you had moments ago, feeling the full weight of your legs, your arms, and the air going into your lungs.

Sit a little longer, and notice any words that come to you after you've arrived at the *blank screen*.

What do you hear now? What do you hear in yourself after the brain has configured how you feel in the moment with memories of every time you've felt this way before?

Perhaps, after being triggered by those aforementioned disruptive statements, your words are "She doesn't know what she is talking about, so why did she write a book about the brain and neuroscience?" or "I knew she was not serious and didn't mean what she said."

Then pause a little longer until you make a decision based on those first words you hear in yourself like "I'm giving her a bad review," or "It's okay, I know she was just creating a trigger."

What do you hear now?

Those words are the basis for your decisions.

Chapter 2
Redefining Self-Esteem

The conventional definition of *self-esteem* is whether you like yourself. I redefine the term as the ability of a child or adult to listen to their first instinctual thought, feeling, or idea and make decisions for themselves. My clients are flabbergasted at this definition of *self-esteem*. They often think they're doing just fine. Many people are not aware of their underlying self-esteem issues, and aren't able to detect when they're reading other people for what they should say or do, or observing others for guidance in their decisions. But still, they generally like themselves, so they consider themselves as the kind of people who have high self-esteem. Needless to say, they are very surprised when I tell them that self-esteem isn't whether you like yourself or not, but your ability to make decisions by listening to your *own* feelings, thoughts, and ideas rather than someone else's.

> Self-esteem isn't whether you like yourself or not, but your ability to make decisions by listening to your *own* feelings, thoughts, and ideas rather than someone else's

Embracing my definition of *self-esteem* will enable you to reverse low self-esteem and become someone who is listening to their own first feelings or first reads of situations and following through with their own ideas to make decisions. Once you've developed my definition of *self-esteem* with the method of *dropping to the blank screen*, you will find that other people will stop being disruptive and start respecting you.

How does that happen?

Well, our first opportunity to develop self-esteem (or lack thereof) happens in childhood. Consider these examples of parents' responses to their children's feeling reactions in the first five years of brain development.

Family 1

"Johnny's hitting me over the head," the child complains.

The parent empathizes. "Oh, I know how that feels."

The child thinks, *There's nothing wrong with me. My parent feels that way, too.*

Or the child walks in the house and notices it's tense. They say, "Hey, Mom, it's tense in here."

The parent says, "Absolutely. Dad and I are working on taxes. This has nothing to do with you. We'll work it out."

The child walks away thinking, *My read of the situation was right.*

Or the child says, "Hey, Mom, I want to build a kite that looks like the Washington Monument."

The parent says, "Oh, interesting idea. Let's go to the store and get the materials. Then you can let me know if you need any help."

What happens to that child?

In the first five years of brain development, they get enough reinforcement every time they feel, observe, or want to try something. That child, over those five years, learns to listen to how they feel, what they observe, and what they want to do. They emerge into adulthood trusting the way they feel, trusting their read of situations, plotting a course for themselves accordingly, and listening to and following through with their ideas.

Family 2

In opposition, there's another type of parenting approach which children experience where their feelings, thoughts, or ideas are not reinforced. Keep in mind that we don't blame parents because they learned this style of parenting from their parents. Here is an example.

The child complains, "Johnny was hitting me over the head."

The parent says, "Well, why didn't you punch him in the nose? What's wrong with you? What did you do wrong?"

The child, instead of noticing how they feel, is filled with disruption. They think, *I should have done something different. I should have known to punch him in the nose. I should have known what Dad told me to do*. And they start second-guessing how they feel instead of noticing how they feel.

Likewise, the same child walks into the house, and says, "Hey, Mom, you look worried."

Their mom says, "Oh no, no, no! I'm not worried. Everything's fine." The child wonders, *What's wrong with me? I thought she looked worried. There must be something terribly wrong with me.*

Or the child says to their parents, "Hey, I have an idea. I want to build a kite that looks like the Washington Monument."

The parents say, "Oh, great idea. Just do it this way and you'll get first prize."

Instead of going out and experimenting on their own ideas, the child has to flip into following the parents' directions and focusing on the parental goal of getting first prize.

What happens to this child?

In two to five years, they stop listening to themselves and become dependent on carefully reading their loving parents for what they should feel, do, and say. And that's where the problems begin, because that child then grows into adulthood dependent on others to guide their decisions and feelings. They go out into our adult world reading everyone except themselves to identify what they should do, feel, and say.

As a result, they start attracting people who bring them a lot of problems: bosses who tend to dump a lot of work on them, romantic partners who insist they do all the emotional work, or friends who call late at night asking for money.

By the time they are hitting their middle to late twenties, they are imploding under the weight of other people's feelings, needs, and desires. That is the time they start experiencing anxiety, depression, substance abuse, eating disorders, panic disorders, or chronic pain. The list goes on.

If you relate to this, my job is to give you a method to develop high self-esteem. You will learn to listen to your own feelings, observations, and ideas, and you'll feel confident following through with them in a way you didn't learn growing up. When you catch yourself reading people around you, you will pause and *drop to the blank screen*, allowing yourself to respond with how you feel, what you observe, or what you want to do. This newfound self-esteem totally changes the way people read you.

Yes, you read that right. People can unconsciously tell if you have high or low self-esteem. How do they know? Because someone with low self-esteem, who is in the habit of reading others for guidance, will by default defer to the disruptive person. Someone with high self-esteem will make and stand by their own decisions, refusing to let others control them or talk them out of their point of view. The individuals around them will eventually have to respect

> Someone with high self-esteem will make and stand by their own decisions, refusing to let others control them or talk them out of their point of view

them—or at least compromise—instead of trying to control them.

It is very important that, when interacting with other people or dealing with triggering feelings, you pause and listen to your own perspective, then make your own decision regarding what to do. Of course, you may be asking yourself, "Well, how do I *drop to the blank screen* when I'm interacting with other people? I can't find those words fast enough."

Here's the blunt answer: If they have trouble giving you enough time to pause, sit back with yourself, listen to your own thoughts, feelings, or ideas, and then respond, there might be a problem with them. They need an immediate response from you so that they can feel in control. Keep *dropping to the blank screen* and expressing your point of view. They'll eventually realize they can't trigger you and will move on to the next person.

In conclusion, *self-esteem* goes much deeper than whether or not you like yourself, indicating instead how capable you are of looking inward for guidance rather than relying on others to shape your thoughts, feelings, and actions. Developing high self-esteem will transform the way you see yourself, and it will also change the way others see and interact with you. People with low self-esteem tend to attract people who will try to control them. But when you think for yourself and know your own feelings and ideas, you'll attract others with high self-esteem, leading to much more fruitful relationships in every area of your life.

Chapter 3
Overcoming the Critical Voice

We learned about the *critical voice* in Chapter 1. This is the inner dialogue that criticizes you, tells you what to do, or debates you all night long. The critical voice wants to win. It is a control freak. But here's the important thing to remember: The critical voice is not alive. It has no medical or psychiatric degree. It is simply a dialogue in your head that wants to be in control of you. And you can never please it. If you listen to it and do what it wants, it will flip and say, "Why didn't you listen to yourself? Why did you listen to me?" It goes back and forth all day long, taking as much time out of your day as you allow it to.

The critical voice develops during childhood when parents don't reinforce a child's thoughts, feelings, and ideas enough. In Chapter 2 we saw this upbringing make the child dependent on reading their parents for what they should feel, do, and say. But the other result is that the critical voice builds strength as the child moves into adulthood and leaves the family home. "Oh, you don't feel that way, you feel this way," it will say, or "Oh, you don't want to do that, you want to do this." The critical voice will mimic the type of dismissal the child encountered growing up.

It's important to note that the critical voice will attack only the areas that did not get enough reinforcement growing up. If every feeling the child had growing up was supported by the parents, the critical voice would leave them alone.

But imagine if every time they had an idea, the parents took over, directing every step of execution and pressuring the child to achieve perfection or "win first prize." When the child reaches adulthood, the critical voice will come up to take over for the parents:

"Oh, you don't want to do it this way, you want to do it that way."

"You have to get first prize."

"You shouldn't do it that way."

For a case study of the critical voice, we examine Miller's struggle with self-doubt during his graduate studies. When I spoke with Miller, he was hearing an internal critical voice saying, "You're not smart enough to do this work." In order for Miller to rewire the self-doubt his critical voice was evoking, he needed to learn how to *drop to the blank screen*, listen to his own words, and make his own decisions related to his dissertation. What follows is an excerpt from my conversation with him:

Dr. Helen McKibben:

Miller, I'm going to ask you for one example of a time you heard a dialogue in your head that had you second-guess yourself, that was criticizing you, telling you what to do, or debating you all night long.

Miller:

Yeah, so the example that really comes to mind for me is when I recently completed a graduate degree. It took me a while to finally complete it because I was going to school part-time. Leading up into my thesis work, I was just the most critical of myself. I thought that my school was basically letting me get away with my thesis topic, and I hadn't really earned what I had achieved. Even after everything was said and done and I got my degree, for a while I was like, "I don't really deserve this degree." And it just really affected me at that particular moment in time.

Dr. Helen McKibben:

Okay. Well, I'm glad you said "at that particular moment in time," because what I'm going to ask you next is the specific vocabulary your critical voice was using. Give us the dialogue, including its tone of voice and how it's speaking to you.

Miller:

I thought, even after I got my degree, no one would've wanted to hire me in my field. I didn't really deserve to get this degree. I had completed the work, but my level of work wasn't of high enough quality for what I aspire to, I guess.

Dr. Helen McKibben:

And so those were the specific words you were hearing from the critical voice?

Miller:

Yeah.

What's my job? My job is to teach your brain to identify the physical onset of a feeling as quickly as possible and to introduce methodologies to identify and resolve the physiology behind feelings so they don't keep building up and causing difficulty.

Identifying the critical voice is a key to both of those goals.

If you haven't done so already, complete the homework assignment in Chapter 1, designed to determine whether or not you have a critical voice. As you go through that twenty-four-hour period noticing your inner dialogue, don't analyze why it's happening. Don't try to fix it. I simply want you to make conscious what might be automatic and unconscious. Do this every time you are listening to your critical voice.

Once you've finished your homework, come back and read the next installment of my conversation with Miller, a role-play of how he interacted with his critical voice and how he could shift from listening to the critical voice to listening to himself.

Dr. Helen McKibben:

I'm going to interact with you in the way that I just heard that the critical voice interacts with you. I want you to add your own dialogue to the interaction, responding specifically to what the critical voice is saying to you.

Dr. Helen McKibben:

You know, I'm really surprised this school is going to let you get away with getting your advanced education. I mean, you've really done a poor job.

Miller:

Yeah. I mean, um. I did a lot of work to get here. I mean, you know, you should've seen some of the other people.

Dr. Helen McKibben:

Yeah. You may have done work, but you're not going to get a job.

Miller:

Um, I kind of already have started, I guess.

Dr. Helen McKibben:

Yeah, but who's going to hire you?

Miller:

That's a good—that's a good point.

Dr. Helen McKibben:

You barely squeak by with the academics. How are you going to get a job?

Miller:

I mean, that's—that's a very real thing.

Dr. Helen McKibben:

Cut.

In this dialogue, Miller is reinforcing his critical voice instead of replacing that voice with his own point of view. Now that we've heard Miller's conversation with his critical voice, it's time for you to explore yours. Start, as usual, by *dropping to a blank screen* (if you need a refresher, turn to "Introduction: How to Drop to the Blank Screen") so that you can start from a neutral physiological and mental position.

Now that you're at your *blank screen*, close your eyes and think about a moment when you were disrupted by the critical voice, recalling as many details as you can.

> What did it keep saying to you?
> What type of things was it persuading you to do?
> What was the outcome of you listening to your critical voice?

With your eyes still shut, shift your focus and notice where you are physically lit up.

> Has your heart rate gone up?
> Are you gritting your teeth?
> Are you curling your toes?
> Where is a physical reaction occurring from just thinking about what the critical voice said?

Now *drop* back *to the blank screen*. Once you're in neutral again, notice what simple words glide in.

> What do you hear?
> Do you hear something related to your thoughts?

Think about the impact the critical voice has had on your thought process.

> How long did it take before the critical voice got you to do what it wanted?
> How long afterward did the consequence of you listening to the critical voice last? Minutes, days, years?
> And how long did you think about it after it happened?

You may be lighting up again physically as you consider these questions. With your eyes shut, please focus on where that's happening and then *drop* your entire body weight back *to the blank screen* you started with. Feeling the full weight of your legs, your arms, and the air going down into your lungs, notice any ideas that you hear about what you will do differently the next time the critical voice tells you what to do.

> What do you hear now?

Finally, revisit your thought process one final time. Review the consequences of listening to your critical voice: a loss of jobs, relationships, money, income, education, or perhaps something else.

As you think about those costs, notice one more time where you're lit up physically. *Drop* your entire body weight until every area that just lit up goes back *to the blank screen* and your own ideas start gliding in. Pick one of your ideas and make a decision about what you'll do differently next time.

Once you've made a decision, your brain will remember it and automatically implement that decision. That's how you'll permanently resolve those feelings. Remember that when we are triggered to feel—in this case, by a critical voice—the first thing the brain does is light us up biochemically and physically. Noticing exactly where you're lighting up immediately stops you from listening. *Dropping to the blank screen* activates the brain in a way that enables you to hear your own words over those of the critical voice.

> *Dropping to the blank screen activates the brain in a way that enables you to hear your own words over those of the critical voice*

To help Miller get through his self-doubt, I taught him the technique of *dropping to the blank screen* whenever he heard the critical voice. Take a look to see what these conversations with your critical voice can look like when you're *dropping* effectively.

Dr. Helen McKibben:

Every time I say something and you come out of this *blank screen*, your heart rate goes up. You want to say something right away. Your breathing changes. You break out in a sweat. Your first and only job is to shift and notice exactly where you're lighting up physically, then simply *drop to the blank screen* until every physical symptom that lit up goes back to neutral. I don't care how long it takes.

If you say anything to me, it will only be after you're completely at the *blank screen*. And you'll only say the words you hear in yourself, not in a reflexive reaction to anything I'm saying. If I find you responding too quickly, I'm going to say, *"Drop."*

So feel the weight of your legs, arms. Be sure your throat is open enough to feel the air go down into your lungs.

I mean, who are you kidding? You think you're going to finish this graduate degree?

Drop all the way *to the blank screen* and then listen for your words.

Miller:

It did take a bit of time management. I was working a full-time job, but I—

Dr. Helen McKibben:

Drop all the way back *to the blank screen* before you say a word. And when you respond, don't answer my question. Respond with your point of view—what you hear in yourself.

Miller:

So from my point of view, I feel very accomplished in what I've completed.

Dr. Helen McKibben:

Go to the *blank screen*. Listen for your words.

Miller:

Yes, it took me a while, but I went through the entire program and completed my thesis while holding down a full-time job. And it actually was a big achievement.

Dr. Helen McKibben:

Well, maybe you did that, but what's going to happen when you get out into the real world? You think someone's going to hire you?

Drop all the way *to the blank screen* 'til you're listening to your words.

Miller:

Yes, I think I have a lot to offer, and I have been hired in my field.

Dr. Helen McKibben:

Whoa. Yeah. Great memory, right? But it's a different world out there now. You've been in a protected environment. Who says they're going to hire you over someone else?

Drop.

Miller:

I'll just let my work stand out, and that way they'll pick me over the quality of my work.

Dr. Helen McKibben:

Cut.

Once Miller started to make progress in pausing and *dropping* before he responded to the critical voice, I reversed the role-play so he could see how the *drop to the blank screen* looks from the outside. Because at first people think, *Well, I'm dropping too long*, so they rush the process. But with me playing Miller's role, he could see (as will you) that there's no rush at all. It takes as long as it takes.

Dr. Helen McKibben:

This time I'm going to be you, and you're going to be the critical voice. First time, I'm not going to *drop to the blank screen*. Second time, I am.

When you're ready, critical voice, go for it.

Miller:

Your thesis project really doesn't fit into the field that you're studying. A lot of your colleagues in school are doing much higher work than what you're doing.

Dr. Helen McKibben:

What do you mean? I'm one of the top students in the class. I don't understand. Well, why do you think that? Do you think something's wrong with me?

Miller:

Well, you're still not as good at giving presentations as some of the other students in the class.

Dr. Helen McKibben:

Well, maybe not, but I'm an excellent writer. Why are you making me doubt myself? I've always been very confident. What do you mean when you say these things?

Miller:

You're just not good enough.

Dr. Helen McKibben:

Cut.

This time, when I'm triggered to feel, I'm going to shift, notice exactly where I'm lighting up, and *drop to the blank screen* long enough to hear my own point of view. When I'm ready, I'll respond to that, so please go ahead.

Miller:

There's just not enough time. You'll never finish this thesis project.

Dr. Helen McKibben:

I always make time for things that are important for me.

Miller:
> When you get out, though, the full thesis will be pointless. You're going to do something completely different.

Dr. Helen McKibben:
> I've learned not to doubt myself.

Miller:
> Don't you think that choosing a different topic could help you in your future career?

Dr. Helen McKibben:
> I think it's important in life to stay with your point of view and follow through with it, no matter how long it takes for a good outcome.

What Miller noticed, and what I'm hoping you'll notice from this exercise, is that there was a difference in how he ended up feeling in his first interaction as the critical voice versus his second. The first time, when I was responding to everything he said right away, he said he felt a bit flustered but in control of the situation. He was driving the conversation; I was simply reacting. But the second time, when I used *dropping* to cultivate more deliberate replies, Miller noted that he certainly didn't feel in control. He was struggling to come up with criticisms because I wasn't merely addressing what he was saying but providing my own point of view.

Watching me take my time to respond and then speak calmly, refusing to give him the responses he wanted, Miller said that, as my critical voice, he ran out of steam and would've preferred to go find someone else to bother. You can give your own critical voice the same treatment, if you just practice taking all the time you need to *drop to the blank screen*, listen to your inner perspective, and respond accordingly.

What is so important about this method? I've said it before, but it bears repeating: A feeling is not resolved by sitting back, breathing, and relaxing. A feeling is resolved by noticing you've been triggered and riding through it physically. This allows your brain to configure a response based on similar experiences, giving you all the information you need to make your own decision about how to respond. That decision completely resolves the triggered feeling, and you stop thinking about it over and over again. If the critical voice ever tries this routine with you again, the brain will automatically retrieve and implement the idea that you came up with, stopping the critical voice in its tracks, preventing it from attaching itself, and ensuring you aren't retriggered by thinking about the issue over and over again.

To sum up: The critical voice develops when a child is taught to second-guess their thoughts, feelings, and ideas while growing up. If you're grappling with a strong critical voice, you're far from alone. My job is to give you a methodology to practice listening to your thoughts instead of your critical voice by *dropping to the blank screen* to make healthy decisions and resolve your triggered feelings. Just like Miller, you can overcome self-doubt by *dropping to the blank screen* and replacing the critical voice with your own thoughts, feelings, and ideas.

> You can overcome self-doubt by *dropping to the blank screen* and replacing the critical voice with your own thoughts, feelings, and ideas

Chapter 4
Substance Abuse and Managing the Addictive Voice

Over my career, the number one driver I've encountered of addiction is the use of a substance (or substances) to run from the very emotions that individuals need to embrace to make good decisions. My job in working with people with substance abuse disorders is to uncover their emotions and then teach them to identify and manage them, no matter how long they've been running from them. I do this by teaching them to rewire their brains by *dropping to the blank screen.*

If I detect in an intake interview that someone seeking therapy has an addiction (such as to alcohol) that circumvents the way they feel, I will ask them to be evaluated for substance abuse treatment. That is where they can start to learn about identifying and managing their feelings in a group setting while working toward giving up the substance at the same time. When a client has that additional support, I can begin teaching them how to *drop to the blank screen*, which will further enhance their life.

This additional support is a firm prerequisite to my working with an individual overcoming addiction, as the *drop* method will not work by itself. This is because substance use eliminates the memory retrieval necessary for the *drop* methodology to work. If you're under the influence of a substance, your amygdala does not retrieve memories of similar triggered feelings to sort them in the necessary ways for making good decisions. Your brain will not work in the way it's designed to when it comes to identifying and using the way you feel to make decisions.

> Substance use eliminates the memory retrieval necessary for the *drop* methodology to work

In my experience, cutting out the substance is just one of three steps that are very important in a person's recovery:

1. Saving your life: eliminating any substance you are currently dependent on.

2. Going to therapy and uncovering what emotions you are running from.
3. Rewiring the brain through *dropping to the blank screen*, which teaches you how to work through and resolve the feelings you've uncovered in therapy.

Step three, which can be completed successfully only if one and two are already well underway, is where I come in.

Rewiring the Brain after Substance Abuse

How does this work with my clients? I start by giving them the same four homework assignments I gave you in Chapter 1. Let's look at how they apply specifically to managing the addictive voice.

In this case, the first and second homework assignments work together particularly closely. Assignment one is to identify how many times you find yourself up in your head, and assignment two is to observe your particular style of managing feelings. More often than not, people with addictions find themselves up in their heads almost constantly, and frequently, their current management style is to run from their feelings.

It shouldn't come as much of a surprise to learn that, if you're battling addiction, the addiction isn't just to the substance. The addiction is *also* to being up in your head and running from your feelings. Individuals with loud addictive voices spend inordinate amounts of time strategizing about when they'll next be able to indulge their addictions. *What time of day will it happen, how will I get it,* and *when will I feel that relief?* This strategizing puts the feelings on hold until those individuals can actually get the drink or the drug that they need to manage their triggered feelings.

The third homework assignment, you'll recall, is about observing other people who trigger us. If you are struggling with addiction, I add another layer: Observe what happens when others disrupt or trigger you. Is that when cravings surface? Is that when you retreat into thoughts about a substance? Do those thoughts stop the disruption or resolve your triggered feelings?

The fourth and most important homework is to notice exactly where you're lighting up physically when you encounter a disruption, a triggered feeling, or an urge to run away from your emotions.

Are you rolling your eyes?

Do you want to say something?

Did your heart rate go up?

Did you break out in a sweat?

Are you gritting your teeth?

Once you know exactly and uniquely where you first light up when you're triggered to feel by the addictive voice, then you can learn to immediately *drop to the blank screen* instead of running, to listen to your words and go through how you feel, instead of strategizing about that next drink. When you learn how to *drop*, you can use your triggers to make healthy, lasting decisions instead of running from your feelings and finding only temporary relief.

When you're overcoming addiction, *dropping to the blank screen* adds a new neuron track configuration that you weren't using before you began treatment. Eventually, it will become the go-to strategy because it feels better than listening to the addictive voice, running from feelings, or being around disruptive people. And it also feels better than waking up in the morning with a hangover, losing

> When you learn how to *drop*, you can use your triggers to make healthy, lasting decisions instead of running from your feelings and finding only temporary relief

your partner, or any of the many serious consequences of substance abuse.

Introducing the Addictive Voice

You may notice that, in this chapter, I've shifted away from talking about the *critical voice* and focused instead on the *addictive voice*. Like the critical voice, the addictive voice undermines your judgment and overrides your logic, but it approaches this from a slightly different angle. An addictive voice says, "Ah, you can drive tonight. There won't be any cops on the road. There's no way you'll get another DWI," or "Oh, nobody will notice if you're high at the dinner party." If you listen to the addictive voice, you will end up in trouble, looking back afterward and wondering why you didn't listen to yourself. (And often you'll hear your critical voice take over and berate you, too.)

You will never win by engaging with an addictive voice. That is exactly why we use the method of *dropping to the blank screen*. This way, you can identify when you are listening to the addictive voice, because you will recognize the areas in which you light up when it triggers you. Then you can shift, *drop, drop, dropping to the blank screen* until you're feeling the full weight of your legs, the full weight of your arms, and the air going down into your lungs. Eventually, you'll hear *your* words—*your* reality. These are the words you listen to, and they replace the addictive voice.

Let me give you an example. You're in substance abuse treatment, and as you're driving down the road, the addictive voice starts an unwelcome dialogue in your head. "Hey," it says, "there's a liquor store over there. You don't have to buy anything. Just go in and get a lottery ticket."

You're accustomed to listening to the addictive voice, and you like the sound of a lottery ticket, so you turn the wheel into the parking lot. But when you walk into the liquor store, that addictive voice comes up again, saying, "Hey, those cases over there are a great price. You won't touch the stuff. Your wife will just use it for parties. Why don't you get two?"

The addictive voice pushes and pushes until you agree. When you buy the cases of alcohol, it becomes quiet, but only for a moment. As you put the alcohol in your car, it comes back. "You know, there are so many bottles here. No one will miss one."

When you get home with the alcohol, it says, "You know, those counselors probably aren't going to do a urine test on you tomorrow in treatment. You could have just one drink. It'll be out of your system before you know it."

But as soon as you ingest the substance, your critical voice swoops in with a vengeance. "Are you kidding me?" it says. "Now you're going to be kicked out of treatment, because they *will* do a urine test on you. Why didn't you listen to yourself?"

This second-guessing and debating goes on and on and on. When you use a substance, you temporarily avoid the addictive and critical voices, but they come right back.

To really silence the addictive voice, you have to have one methodology for identifying when you're even listening to it, and another to replace the addictive voice with your own voice when you're making decisions. *Dropping to the blank screen* encompasses both of these methodologies.

Retraining Your Brain through Role-Play

Another way to retrain a substance-dependent brain is including role-play in your therapy. This allows you to practice handling a situation where feelings you've wanted to run away from previously have been triggered, disrupting your day or setting your brain on a loop of criticism. As we saw in my role-play with

Miller in Chapter 3, spontaneously reacting to such triggering situations is much different—and much less effective—than taking the time to notice where you're lighting up, *dropping to the blank screen* until those physically activated areas are back to neutral, and then responding with the words you hear coming from yourself. Again, when you are able to respond effectively from the *blank screen*, you'll respond with a stable voice and a confident point of view that ensures the disruptive individual knows they cannot transfer their feelings to you.

Of course, dealing with other people in this way is easier said than done. Often the skill is best learned through role-play, where individuals can replay or practice triggering situations by *dropping to the blank screen* and then deciding how they want to respond. You can do this with a therapist, like Miller did with me, but you can also do a modified version on your own: When you inevitably think back to a triggering situation you handled less effectively than you would have liked, go ahead and take the opportunity to practice your new methodology. Shift, notice where you're lighting up, and *drop to the blank screen* long enough to hear your words. Then decide what you'll say or do differently next time a similar situation arises.

This exercise will empower your brain to completely resolve the feeling. You'll stop thinking about the scenario over and over again, and if the same individuals disrupt you again, your brain will know to automatically retrieve and implement the idea that you came up with, whether it was six minutes ago or six years ago.

Here's an example of a triggering scenario you may have faced in real life or may want to explore in role-play. Imagine you're visiting friends or relatives who know you're in treatment but aren't supporting you. Your brother offers you a beer, saying, "Ah, you'll be fine. You can have a drink. No one will know, and no one's doing urine tests here, anyway."

The offer fills you with disruptive emotions and you begin to second-guess yourself, to consider listening to your brother's argument instead of your own voice. If you don't have the ability to notice the unique signals your body is sending—where you're lighting up—you might take his bait. But if you have a method that allows you to recognize what is happening, then you can *drop to the blank screen*. This sparks your brain to retrieve memories of every time you've been through this before and what's happened as a result of your decisions. With this information in mind, you can listen to what's in your best interest and respond with what *you* need to say or do for yourself. In this case, your response may be, "No, I'm really invested in treatment. I'm going home."

Unfortunately, silencing your brother's voice may not be the end of the battle. External triggers can combine with your addictive and critical voices as well as a habitual desire to run from your feelings. For example, imagine that after you leave your brother's house and get home, your addictive voice chimes in to take his place. "Oh, you'll be fine. You can drink." Maybe your critical voice adds, "Why were you so lame back there? Your brother was just trying to have some fun."

All of a sudden you're up in your head, running from your feelings as you strategize where to go for some alcohol, what to buy, and when to drink it. If you don't *drop to the blank screen* as each of these voices and tendencies crop up, you're liable to relapse. And even if you don't succumb by starting to drink right away, these thoughts will occupy your mind, growing in volume and intensity until you stop them—either temporarily with booze, or more effectively with a measured response derived from a *drop to the blank screen.*

Another thing to pay attention to when you're overcoming addiction is how your addictive voice can be triggered in completely unrelated situations, such as the workplace. Here's another scenario to inspire your role-play exercises: Imagine you're a teacher and you have a student who really gets under your skin. Your addictive voice may have you counting down the hours till class is over and you can have a drink to take the edge off. But in reality, that response won't solve anything. You'll be facing a relapse, and the child will be just as "spirited" tomorrow.

Rather, the quickest way to fix the situation for good is to show the child that they can't get under your skin. How? You guessed it: by noticing where you're lighting up and *dropping to the blank screen* until those physically activated areas go back to neutral. Then you'll be ready to respond to the child in a confident (and compassionate) way that will show them they cannot control you.

For another example, imagine your sister calls for an immediate response to a tough question. She's transferring her anxiety onto you, and if you take the bait, you're opening the door for your addictive voice to make an unwelcome visit. But if you have the ability to notice where you're lighting up, you can shift and *drop to the blank screen* long enough for your brain to configure your point of view and respond in a way that flips the disruption back to your sister. She walks away knowing she has to manage her own feelings. In both scenarios—the child at school and the sister at home—*dropping to the blank screen* before you respond enables you to do two things:

1. Avoid the temptation to run from your feelings and toward a substance.
2. Pre-empt that triggered addictive and/or critical voice from recurring again tomorrow.

Preparing for a Lifelong Journey

Of course, overcoming addiction is a long-term battle, and as much as I wish I could say once is enough, the truth is that you will be triggered over and over again in treatment and in everyday life. You will be practicing this technique repeatedly for many years. Here's the important thing, though: Your approach doesn't have to be perfect to be a good start. I don't care how far you initially get in the process—if you remember to shift and notice where you're lighting up, but you forget to *drop to the blank screen* and access your words, you've taken a step. And that next piece will eventually happen with practice. If you do *drop to the blank screen*, and then that addictive voice comes in again, you haven't failed. You just have to shift again, notice where you're lit up, and *drop to the blank screen* again until you can stay there long enough to replace the addictive voice with your own.

If you forget to do any of it, your brain is so beautifully designed that it will keep bringing up the memory of the trigger afterward, giving you ample opportunity to practice these techniques until you get to the point where you can hear your fully developed ideas so you can make your own decisions and resolve those feelings for good. Next time, your brain will automatically retrieve and implement the decision that you previously made in practice. Every time it will get just a little easier to say, "No thanks, I don't want to drink this time." That is what treatment is all about.

Chapter 5
Disordered Eating and How the Brain Guides What We Eat

Memory retrieval is very involved in our food choices. The way our brains guide what we eat—whether those patterns are healthy or disordered—is established in the early years of development. As we get older, our brains will make choices based on memories of the foods that we were used to eating while growing up.

At the most basic level, the brain guides these patterns by recognizing—and then asking for—what the body needs. For example, your brain is designed to advise if your body needs certain levels of liquid or nutrients. If the brain notes that liquid levels are below the necessary levels, it will automatically trigger a craving for liquids. If it notes a deficiency in a particular nutrient, it will trigger a craving for something that's high in that nutrient—perhaps a craving for lemonade because the brain is telling of dehydration or a need for some vitamin C. If you crave chocolate milk, your brain may be signaling that calcium levels are low.

These nutrition-based cravings are almost comically obvious during pregnancy. We laugh at jokes about how women want crazy things when they are pregnant, but even the classic "pickles and ice cream" combo is not so crazy. Think about it like this: The expectant mother is being drained of calcium in the process of developing a baby, so of course she's going to want or need dairy to help replenish it. And her sodium levels are affected by pregnancy, too, so even if she's never really loved them before, she may start craving pickles or potato chips to make up the deficit. Pickles and ice cream may sound like a strange combination, but you can't argue with that kind of reasoning from the brain.

Along with meeting our nutritional needs, our brains are wired to suggest eating patterns based on our emotional needs—though these patterns, as you may imagine, are often less about what's healthy and more about our feelings. In fact, much like the critical voice, these patterns have a lot to do with whether a child's thoughts, feelings, and ideas are supported as they're growing up. Consider a child who's turned off by the gooey whites the first time he encounters scrambled eggs on his breakfast plate. If that child is growing up in an environment where his parents are supporting him, listening not only to what he hears in himself but his decisions, then the next time he goes down in the morning and sees scrambled eggs, he's going to recall how he felt about them last time and confidently say, "No, thanks. I want cereal."

On the other hand, a child whose parents control every aspect of their eating—or cast judgment on what or how much they eat—will lose their confidence to eat intuitively, instead developing a strong critical voice that makes them second-guess every meal (more on that later).

Cultivating Food Memories

Our brains create and resurface these memories for us as adults, too, if we let them. Think about the last time something you ate made you ill. Maybe you were at a restaurant offering food that's foreign to you, or maybe it was a tuna on rye at your local lunch counter. Next time you're faced with food choices that include those items, if you *drop to the blank screen* or notice when your memory is triggered, you will know what foods *not* to choose. But if you haven't developed a style of noticing you're being triggered and *dropping* long enough to retrieve those memories, you may find yourself going back to those trigger foods—and the subsequent illness—over and over again.

Dropping to the blank screen enhances the decision-making work our brains are already doing based on our memories and experience. If we don't *drop to the blank screen* every time we're triggered to feel—including whatever we may be feeling about food—we will continue to make the same old choices that don't serve us well. *Dropping to the blank screen* is designed to enable us to listen to ourselves in reality, reflect on our memories of what happened to us in the past, and make healthy decisions accordingly.

Remember that the three factors behind our food choices tend to be what we ate growing up, what the brain alerts us to regarding nutritional needs, and what memories we have of positive and negative food experiences. Those three categories fit beautifully together because when you *drop to*

> The three factors behind our food choices tend to be what we ate growing up, what the brain alerts us to regarding nutritional needs, and what memories we have of positive and negative food experiences

the blank screen, your brain is retrieving everything it knows about each of those areas, combining all that information in nanoseconds to spit out ideas of how and what to eat to feel good rather than bad—physically and mentally. This mechanism for both noticing when we're triggered and retrieving memories of prior responses empowers us to make good decisions about the way we eat.

Overcoming Disordered Eating Habits

This isn't just about what foods we like or what makes us sick. It's also about overcoming disordered eating patterns and behaviors. Take binging, for example. If I eat a whole pizza one night, and I wake up to find the rings on my fingers are tight, and my waistband is tight, I won't like the way I feel. That is an outcome my brain will file away as a memory. The next time I want a pizza, if I *drop to the blank screen* and retrieve that memory, I'm much more likely to decide to eat just a couple slices and save the rest for later. On the flip side, if I'm tempted to "save some calories" by skipping breakfast one morning, *dropping to the blank screen* will give me an opportunity to recall that, the last time I skipped breakfast I was sluggish all day, struggled at work, and ended up ordering fast food for dinner on the way home. By using that memory, it's much easier to decide to make a smoothie or grab a granola bar instead of skipping breakfast.

Two factors in particular are present in disordered eating patterns: our upbringings and the distractions we face. Let's talk first about upbringings, and we'll start with caretakers who might unconsciously pass on their disordered eating habits to the child. Consider a child whose caretaker says things like "Oh, you don't want to eat that," or "You'll never be as skinny as your girlfriends if you eat that."

Those types of comments take away the child's agency and reinforce negative emotions around food. A child may think, *Well, I wanted to eat that, but they said it would be bad for me.* Sooner or later, the child will grow to second-guess their own natural instincts about how much or what they want to eat—cookies and salads alike.

Another type of upbringing that can lead to unhealthy eating patterns is one in which parents who are health-food advocates impose a lot of restrictions on what a child eats, praising some foods and vilifying others. The child doesn't get to eat Twinkies like everyone else at lunch, and they grow up desperate to try something they've been taught is "bad."

Eventually, they start hiding those "bad" foods and eating them in secret, and by the time they're grown up and the parents are gone, they'll eat a whole box of Twinkies, leading to both an upset stomach and an upset mind. The way a child's parents respond to their cravings and curiosities around food is very important in planting healthy eating habits for the future.

The other big-picture issue that often contributes to unhealthy or disordered eating is distractors, and these come in a variety of forms. TV commercials are designed to trigger us to crave particular foods or beverages, and listening to those advertisements can often distract us from our own nutritional goals.

Another distractor is other people. A friend's invitation to a barbecue might be tempting even though you've been avoiding red meat to lower your cholesterol. But if you give in to pleasing your friend instead of doing what's right for you, your critical voice will certainly have something to say about it. If, however, you notice you're lit up by the question of going to the barbecue, you can *drop to the blank screen* long enough to retrieve the information that will encourage you to say, "Thanks for the invite, but I'm staying with my current eating regimen, because I feel so much better," or "I'll be there, but will fill up on sides instead of ribs." At the end of the night—and likely the next morning, too—you'll feel better, both physically and mentally, thanks to the informed, self-confident choice you made.

The third—and often biggest—distraction is the critical voice, which will replicate the types of messages about food choices you may have received growing up. "Oh, you don't want to eat that," or "No, you want to look like Susie, so you shouldn't eat this." Again, if a child's preferences and decisions are not supported when they want to eat a food or when they don't, the child will become dependent on other people, or on their critical voice, to make the choices for them.

When we're talking about an eating disorder, I believe that the critical voice and the messages the child heard growing up are two of the biggest culprits in perpetuating harmful habits. Those who struggle with eating disorders like anorexia or bulimia are also in a constant struggle with the critical voice and memories from their upbringings (familial, societal, or both) as they debate how much they should eat or not eat. To complicate things further, individuals struggling with eating disorders are often up in their heads, running from their feelings by strategizing about their eating. (This can be similar to other addictions.)

So if you're someone battling disordered eating and this one-two punch of a critical voice telling you what you should and should not eat, and you have a habit of strategizing incessantly about food, you need a methodology that puts you in a position to make decisions based on your own perspective and experience.

If you can rewire your brain to stop listening to the critical voice, stop running from feelings, and to listen to yourself consistently, you will be able to resolve those triggered feelings and walk away, making strides in healing your relationship to food. No longer are you thinking (or strategizing or stressing) constantly about food. Instead, you choose your food, you ingest it, you notice how you feel, and you go on with your day.

If you enter into treatment for an eating disorder, or you are struggling with disordered eating, you'll encounter three goals. Just like with addiction treatment, they always occur in the same order. The goals are:

1. Save your life. In this phase, your providers will make the decisions for you

about what you will eat and when. This first step is critical because, if your brain isn't receiving the nutrients necessary to function properly, it's not going to retrieve memories that are as effective in decision-making.
2. Understand the emotions behind the disorder. This work, which usually involves therapy, allows the individual to identify and go through the very feelings they've been running from.
3. Rewire the brain. Once you've worked through step one and are working on step two, you have to learn how to make healthy food choices for yourself based only on what your body really needs.

If you don't continue to practice what you learned in those three components of treatment, you may relapse and have to go through the whole cycle again. As with overcoming addiction, this is a long-term practice, but one you absolutely have the power to undertake.

Understanding Internal and External "Food Critics"

My interview subject, J.R., wasn't coming to me for support with disordered eating, but he did have some hang-ups about his eating—or, rather, how others perceived his eating. This excerpt from a conversation I had with him is a good way to see the impact that a critical inner voice, memories from upbringing, and external distractions could have on our eating patterns, if we let them.

J.R.:

The biggest thing with my eating habits is that I eat very quickly. It has become a socially unacceptable issue. For example, I'll go to a restaurant with my friends and the waiter will say, "Oh, you ate that quickly. You must have been hungry." And it happens a lot.

Dr. Helen McKibben:

What do you remember from the first time you noticed you had to eat quickly?

J.R.:

It was probably the first time I ate a meal at boarding school. At boarding school, we were given only about twenty minutes to eat. There wasn't a lot of food available, and we were all competing for it with a bunch of other men. It just became natural. Everybody else was eating quite quickly, and I was eating slowly. Then I realized the seconds were already gone. At that point, it was almost a survival mechanism. But then, all of my friends were doing it, too.

Dr. Helen McKibben:

What happened when you grew into a young adult and an individual made this comment to you?

J.R.:

It wasn't one individual who would make comments about how quickly I was eating. It was fairly consistent. It was people who were not my friends or associates or co-workers. It was people I had never met before who were in the food service industry.

I had never gotten this sort of comment before when I was in boarding school. None of my friends or peers, or even my family, said I ate too quickly. It was outsiders looking at me, and it made me definitely question *Am I eating too quickly?* I never thought I was, but I do know I eat much faster than everybody else.

But I also enjoy those memories of eating quickly and then being able to talk to my friends in that very limited amount of time we had. When I was younger, it was seen as a positive. But now I'm getting negative feedback.

Dr. Helen McKibben:

This is an example of being disrupted by other individuals, like in your third homework assignment.

When you notice that an individual's comment is lighting you up, then it's time to *drop to the blank screen* long enough for that physical area to go back to neutral, which activates recall so you can make decisions about how to respond based on what your brain puts together from your memories about eating fast. That would be your decision-maker.

J.R.:

I want to eat how I'm going to eat. These people don't know me, and they will never be my friends. Maybe they have issues they're trying to project on me? But it does create very awkward social situations.

Dr. Helen McKibben:

What we know about the brain is that, if you have the ability to pause when triggered, then *drop* and listen to yourself, you will make choices based on memory recall and what feels good. And obviously what felt really good was the companionship and the time to visit with your friends, so you didn't mind the way you were eating. A healthy brain will adapt to the eating styles that make you comfortable or bring up pleasant memories, not the ones that simply please other people.

J.R.:

Could it be because I don't place such a high value on eating? And the people who are criticizing me do? The speed they eat and what they eat never even enters my mind.

Dr. Helen McKibben:

People who disrupt us may not be doing it consciously. They might have had someone in their upbringing who controlled what they ate in the way they were trying to control you. We often find that people reenact with others the way they were treated growing up.

Dieting

Before we move away from disordered eating, let's talk about dieting in general, as the line between the two can be elusive and incredibly faint. Many diet programs restrict the type of foods available, offering limited choices. Remember the child who grew up with serious food restrictions? The same principle applies to adults. If an individual is restricted by a diet program from the type of foods their brain is craving (due to childhood memories or from nutritional necessity), they will not use that diet program for very long. And beyond that, they'll likely fall into a harmful "binge and restrict" pattern that does far more harm than good, because the brain and its cravings are going to win out over the eating decisions someone else is requiring of them.

If you're going to follow a diet plan, please choose one that allows plentiful food choices and empowers you to decide for yourself what to eat and when. Those are the plans that will best incorporate how your brain is designed to make decisions about food or beverages, and those plans will be more effective than highly restrictive ones.

Here's an analogy about the importance of making food choices that agree with you and your brain. Have you ever joined a gym because a friend recommended it, then (after committing to only a year of membership, of course) found that they did not have the activities you liked? Maybe they didn't have a pool, or all they had was weight-training equipment and no bicycles. When you signed up for that membership, you were up in your head, painting a picture of how you were going to lose weight or build an exercise habit. But because you didn't *drop to the blank screen* and incorporate your own experience of what you like to do for exercise, you committed to a plan that didn't work for you. You likely won't continue to use that gym, meaning you've wasted money and set yourself back a year in working toward your health goals. You beat yourself up, wondering, *Why am I not going to this gym?*

Well, there's a reason: When you were a child, you liked to ride bicycles, not lift weights. Or you currently like swimming instead of doing aerobics. Whether you're choosing a gym membership or a healthy-eating plan, be sure to do so after *dropping* long enough for your brain to retrieve memories about what you like and what works for your body.

Incorporating your point of view into your food plans is paramount, and that includes retrieving memories about food choices that work and do not work for you so you can identify a food plan that allows you to listen to yourself first. Just like the gym whose offerings work best for the friend who recommended it, remember that

> Incorporating your point of view into your food plans is paramount

every food plan or diet book worked for the individual who wrote it. It was written based on *their* upbringing and *their* memory recall, not yours. We can all buy a lot of diet plans, but maybe what we really need to do is write our own diet books.

Ultimately, your brain is your best diet plan. The most effective food plan is your ability to *drop to the blank screen* and let your brain put together every experience you've had with eating, identifying what worked for you and what didn't. Once you listen to that perspective—your perspective—and make a decision, your brain will recall what works for you every time you are triggered to want to eat something. By doing that, you are rewiring your brain for healthy food decision-making.

This applies to weight-loss apps and exercise- or calorie-tracking apps too. They're only useful if you're using them to make your own decisions about food choices by *dropping to the blank screen*. Apps that work even better are the ones which incorporate emotions along with food choices. That would set you up to identify and go through the emotions that are triggered when you want to eat a certain food. Once you've done that, the choices you make will include memory retrieval of what's worked for you before, how you've ended up feeling before, and what works best with your body and brain. Similarly, apps that ask you to journal your food choices and emotions will work only if you *drop to the blank screen* and fill out those journal entries intentionally. If you simply write without going through your feelings, then the journal can become a tool for running from feelings instead of feeling them. Journaling is wonderful if you identify and *drop* through the triggered feelings before you write.

To reiterate, you don't need to track your emotions in an app to lose weight. Such apps become useful when you use the data they collect to make your own decisions about food choices, rather than letting an app dictate what, when, and how much you eat. The app isn't in control of you.

Making Healthy Choices for Life

From diets to disordered eating to just eating in a way that makes us feel good, we need to rewire our brains to make healthy food choices by learning to *drop to the blank screen* and examine the variables driving those choices: what our brains are pushing us to crave out of necessity, the food habits learned during our upbringing, and how certain foods make us feel.

It's not the amount of food, but the obsession or constant thought about food that takes you away from good decision-making. If you don't make decisions, you don't change your brain. If you don't *drop to the blank screen*, you don't make good decisions, period.

Chapter 6
Getting Sleep and Using Your Dreams to Resolve Feelings

One of the things happening when we avoid feelings all day long is that the physiology of those feelings continues to build. By the time your head hits the pillow and you want to fall asleep, you may find yourself unable to stop thinking, too restless to sleep.

What does the brain need to go to sleep?

You may say melatonin, relaxation, breathing techniques, a drink, or a drug. They could all help, but that's not where I'm going. I'll give you a clue.

Think about what an individual receives when they visit a sleep specialist. Not just medication but a CPAP machine that floods the upper respiratory tract with massive amounts of oxygen. What a brain needs to go to sleep is not melatonin or medication but increased oxygen to induce the natural chemicals necessary for sleep, just like with a CPAP machine.

And what inhibits oxygen and blood flow to the brain? Continuing to think about issues that are bothering you when your head hits the pillow. Those thoughts cause neuromuscular reactions that decrease oxygen flow to the brain. If you go up into your thought process and try to divert yourself by counting sheep or talking yourself through breathing exercises or progressive relaxation techniques, you will often go back to the worrying and predicting you were doing before, because you haven't resolved the issues that were bothering you—you've only pushed them away.

Think of some of the things you have tried to use to go to sleep: apps that play ocean noises, recordings that instruct you to relax your body one part at a time, or apps that talk you through relaxation exercises. All of those things are techniques to reduce the physical buildup of triggered feelings that we can end up with at the end of the day, but they don't go fast enough or far enough to maximize oxygen flow to your brain as quickly as possible.

What you need is a purely physical method of resolving those thoughts. When you can't stop thinking about a subject or a situation, you can shift, notice where you're lighting up, and *drop to the blank screen* long enough for that physically activated area to go back to neutral. Then you will produce enough oxygen flow to go to sleep. If there are a lot of issues building up during the day or thoughts that jump on board when you shut your eyes at night, all you need to do is *drop to the blank screen.*

If you start thinking about those things again, *drop* again. You may have to repeat the exercise twenty or twenty-five times, but eventually, usually within about ten minutes, you will receive enough oxygen flow to the brain and you will be asleep. Your difficulty going to sleep isn't an analytic issue. It's an oxygen-flow issue, and I'm going to show you how to overcome it.

But first, think about the last time you had difficulty getting to or staying asleep.

What were you thinking about? What type of things did you do to get to sleep? What was the outcome? Just think for a moment about that example.

Before I teach you my techniques for *dropping* yourself to sleep, I'll give you a couple of examples that illustrate what we're up against when our thoughts keep us awake at night. Have you ever been in a situation where you stayed up all night long, thinking about the fact that you couldn't go to sleep? *Oh, I'm going to get seven-and-a-half hours of sleep,* you may have thought when you turned off the light. But as time went by your thoughts were, *Now it's six hours and five minutes. Oh no, and now it's four hours.*

The reason that happens is because each thought that has a feeling or worry attached is also accompanied by a physiological reaction, and those neuromuscular contractions build and decrease oxygen flow to the brain. Every time you thought about how many hours of sleep you were or weren't getting, it triggered a physical reaction that built up and squeezed off oxygen and blood flow to your brain. What you need is a methodology that increases oxygen flow to the brain.

Three Techniques to Summon Sleep

The next time you're having difficulty getting to sleep, try one of these three techniques. I promise they're far more effective than counting sheep.

1. Drop to the Blank Screen

The first technique is to notice what you can't stop thinking about when your head hits the pillow. Shift to noticing instead where whatever you're thinking about is lighting you up physically. Then *drop to the blank screen* until those thoughts stop. When you're at the *blank screen*, your brain is getting maximum oxygen flow, which is exactly what it needs to go to sleep. (If you need a refresher on what *dropping to the blank screen* looks like, remember that you can always turn back to "Introduction: How to Drop to the Blank Screen.")

To practice this technique, think back to the last time you couldn't sleep. Where did you light up? What were you sleeping on? What was the temperature of your pillow as you tossed and turned? What were you thinking about? As you revisit the details, *drop*, let all of that go, and imagine the oxygen rushing to your brain to lull you to sleep.

2. Focus on the Darkness

The second technique you may want to use when you're up in your head and you can't stop thinking goes as follows: Notice if you have *repetitive* thoughts, meaning you're lighting up in the same ways over and over. Close your eyes, and shift instead to looking at the darkness behind your closed eyelids, inspecting the shapes of any visible light.

Allow your eyes to drift back and down. You will notice you are automatically back at that *blank screen*, feeling the full weight of your torso, legs, and arms, feeling the air going down into your lungs. You don't have to talk your body into anything because this is where you need to be, at the *blank screen*, for the brain to fall asleep.

Eyes still shut, think again about the last time you couldn't sleep. How long did it take 'til you finally got to sleep? How long did you try various techniques until you actually fell asleep? How long did your sleeplessness affect you the following day? Notice, as you become more skilled at *dropping*, how those time frames shorten with each repetitive thought you resolve.

3. Notice How Your Thoughts Change

A third technique you could use is to shift from thinking or ruminating when you shut your eyes to noticing how quickly or slowly one thought changes to the next. Notice how often one thought merges into the next or how often and quickly the brain keeps rotating. Instead of listening to the content of your thoughts, notice their rhythm instead. This shift stops you from listening to the thoughts that would otherwise build up in a way that could cause physical reactions in your body. Stopping this spiral allows the autonomic nervous system to *drop to the blank screen* automatically. Again, no thinking is required, because this is where you need to be for your brain to go to sleep.

Dropping into Dreams

One of the things that happens with the use of substances to fall asleep is that they temporarily reduce the physiological response associated with feelings that have built up over the course of the day. You get a temporary hit of oxygen and your brain goes to sleep, but then it wakes up again. The reason is that using a drink or a drug doesn't allow the brain to get to restorative stage of sleep where dreams occur, which is necessary to resolve feeling states.

If you do not get restorative sleep, you do not dream, and dreaming is the brain's brilliant way of configuring facts and details in ways that force you into the feeling states you avoided during your waking hours. Dreams force you to go ahead and feel triggered feelings in a safe, rested state.

Dreaming, in other words, is a natural way of *dropping to the blank screen*. If you don't get REM

(Rapid Eye Movement) sleep, you don't process those feelings, and you don't sleep through the night, either. If you get REM sleep, the brain forces you to go through your unresolved feelings so you can wake up in the morning refreshed.

REM sleep is where the brain does the emotional work for you. It is brilliantly designed to have you go through feelings, both physically and emotionally, to full resolution. If you ever wake up questioning the details of your dream, don't try to analyze what the dream means. Instead, notice what feelings it pushes you to feel. That is more important, and the answer to that question will give you a good idea about what feelings were left unresolved the day before.

> Don't try to analyze what the dream means. Instead, notice what feelings it pushes you to feel

In fact, analyzing your feelings is just another way to get stuck in your head and run from your feelings. For example, if you keep having dreams about tornadoes or your teeth falling out, there's no need or reason to figure out, literally, what that means. What's more important is to pause and recall the feelings the dream was pushing you through—the fear of your teeth falling out or the anxiety around the coming tornado. I promise you, it's not about a tornado, and it's not about your teeth. It's about the feelings of anxiety or fear that you did not process during the day. The brain is beautifully designed to use sleep to help you process those feelings.

Dropping Yourself to Sleep

If you're having trouble sleeping at night, I propose that you shift and notice if you're lit up anywhere. I can almost guarantee that you'll notice feelings that you need to work through by *dropping to the blank screen*. Even if you have to *drop* several times, this practice will get your brain enough oxygen flow to send you to dreamland. But again, once you're there, remember: If you go up in your head to figure out what your dream is about, you're back in your thought process where you're going to start spinning out, worrying, predicting, or listening to the critical voice. The way to get back to sleep is not to think; it is to neutralize any lit-up or physically activated areas and get that maximum oxygen flow back to your brain. It isn't an issue of figuring out the details; it's an issue of resolving the feelings that the brain wants you to deal with.

To recap, I have given you three techniques that will get you to REM sleep:

1. Notice what you can't stop thinking about, and shift instead to notice where you're lit up and *drop to the blank screen.*
2. Notice what you can't stop thinking about, and instead shift to notice the darkness behind your closed eyelids, inspecting the shapes of light. Allow your eyes to drift back and down, which automatically takes you back to the *blank screen.*
3. Notice thought rhythms: how quickly or slowly each thought is occurring or how quickly or slowly each stops and starts or rotates to the next thought, releasing the autonomic nervous system physically and taking you back to the *blank screen.*

These three techniques will work beautifully to resolve the physiology and the underlying emotions you didn't deal with during your waking hours, enabling you to get enough oxygen flow to your brain to naturally go to sleep. Don't talk yourself to sleep. *Drop* yourself to sleep.

Chapter 7
External Disruptors: Dealing with Difficult People

So far, we have been talking about internal disruption. But many external disruptions occur in life. Some of the things that trigger us more than anything else are our experiences with other people. Often, when we interact with people, we walk away regretting what we have said or done. As we've seen in previous chapters, we sometimes feel disrupted in a way we simply hadn't before the interaction occurred.

Why does this happen? Because you are among the many who aren't dealing with their feelings, and when others identify you as someone they can knock off balance or out of control, they will interact with you in such a way that they transfer their own triggered feelings to you.

In this chapter, I'll teach you how to use the *drop* methodology to identify when this is happening, and how to block it by listening to your own thoughts, feelings, and ideas before responding.

Why is that so important? Because when you pause and listen to your point of view instead of immediately reacting to what someone is saying or immediately responding to their questions, the other individual will recognize that you can't be knocked off balance and they'll stop trying. It is very important when interacting with other people that they recognize you're not immediately catering to them. You want them to know that you're pausing, listening to yourself, and thinking it through for yourself before you respond. This makes it clear that they can't control you. Of course, they may not take the hint right away; they may try consciously or subconsciously several times to disrupt you by upping the ante because they expect to knock you off balance easily, whether because of your age or because they've interacted with similar people before. But if you stand your ground, eventually one of two things will happen. Either they'll find someone else to disrupt with their unresolved feelings, or, even better, they'll start respecting you because they can't knock you off balance, opening the door to reciprocal communication.

Dropping to the blank screen when others are being disruptive isn't just to resolve your anxiety or tension. Just like when you *drop to the blank screen* in any of the situations we've already discussed, your brain will quickly configure memories of every time you've felt this way before, what's happened, what's worked in those situations, what hasn't worked in them, and what works for you. In a matter of nanoseconds, the brain spits out simple words or ideas of what you could say so you don't keep feeling those old ways again. When you take action based on this analysis and walk away from the interaction, having responded from your point of view, you resolve the feeling completely, pre-empting your critical voice from bringing up the situation over and over again afterward, demanding, "Why didn't you say this?" or "Why didn't you say that?"

Dropping in Your Professional Life

Dropping to the blank screen can be helpful with disruptive people in your personal life, but it can also have a powerful impact on your professional success. To illustrate how this technique might work in the workplace, I spoke with sales expert Jacob who subtly uses the *dropping* technique to foster better relationships with prospects.

Dr. Helen McKibben:

Jacob, as a salesperson, how do you provide value or get through to someone who has already decided they don't want to hear what you have to say?

Jacob:

What I try to do with every call is relate to whoever I'm on the phone with, and that can definitely be very difficult given their industry knowledge or their seniority. But there's always a way to relate to somebody, whether that be their hometown, what's been going on in their industry, or what has been going on in the world. It's not that hard to try to connect with somebody.

What is hard is when you attempt that connection and get shot down over and over again. Maybe by the tenth time, the person will respond well, but we are wired to avoid failure, so it's not easy to persist that long. That's why sales is difficult: you're going to fail so many more times than you succeed, to the factor of thousands.

When really thinking about what you can give somebody on the other end of the phone in the current moment, that's positive regard, empathy, and respect. I think that no matter how someone reacts to you, you can strike a chord with them by responding positively.

Dr. Helen McKibben:

One of the things that we focus on with *dropping to the blank screen* is that if you respond immediately to other people, they can often read that you're trying to please them. If, however, you pause and then come back with honesty or empathy, that sets them up to listen to what you have to say. Have you ever experienced that?

Jacob:

Absolutely. Especially in sales. Often you have to assume a lot in sales, and you get used to hearing a prospect say, "No, that's not what I handle at all," or "That's not my area." I can't stumble and say, "Oh, but wait, wait, wait, wait, hear me out," because they're going to hang up.

But I'm much more likely to be successful if I take a second to show I'm listening to them, thinking of a new approach based on my own experience, even if that's simply, "Who does handle that within your organization, and what are the chances I could get a conversation with them?"

Dr. Helen McKibben:

That would set them up to be curious about what you're going to say, that pause. If you're in the field of sales, Jacob, how do you show that you care without being a people-pleaser or trying to get them to do what you want?

Jacob:

I think it starts with mirroring and expanding on what they've said, not in terms of *reacting*, but thoughtfully and intentionally repeating and either expanding on the feelings conveyed or expressing your interpretation of what they may have meant. It's not about just giving them the one-word answer they were hoping to get.

Oftentimes, you mirror someone's tone of voice or reflect back what you know is going on in their world in order to get them to listen. By that, I mean, if somebody answers the phone frantically and you start to have a very calm dialogue with them, they're not going to respond well to that.

If you say something like, "Oh my gosh, sounds like you're tremendously busy right now. What's going on?" they might be willing to tell you about it. A lot of times people don't get the chance to talk about themselves, and being able to differentiate yourself in that way definitely gives you the ability to deal with an unruly or a very difficult customer.

Everything Jacob is talking about here requires learning to pause, *drop to the blank screen*, listen to the memories your brain retrieves about previous experiences, and respond accordingly. It takes more thought and effort than simply reacting in the moment, but this technique will always drive better long-term results.

To see what it would look like to use the *drop* technique with someone who's already decided that they don't want to respond to what he's selling, I did a role-play exercise with Jacob. We did the exercise twice. The first time, rather than *dropping* and responding thoughtfully, I asked Jacob to simply plow ahead with his pre-planned script and off-the-cuff reactions. As you may imagine, he didn't get very far. Here's an excerpt.

Dr. Helen McKibben:
Hello?

Jacob:
Hi, Helen. I wanted to talk with you about some software that really can help you with your HIPAA compliance. Did you have a minute to talk?

Dr. Helen McKibben:
> I don't know.

Jacob:
> Would right now work?

Dr. Helen McKibben:
> I'm going to have to look at my schedule. I'm pretty busy.

Jacob:
> Is it in front of you right now?

Dr. Helen McKibben:
> I'd have to get my secretary to look at it.

Jacob:
> All right. Well, have you ever heard of software that can help with HIPAA compliance and automate a lot of the regulatory things you have to do?

Dr. Helen McKibben:
> I don't know. I'm really thinking about something else right now.

Then we tried again, and this time Jacob took the time he needed to *drop to the blank screen* and respond intentionally to what he was hearing from me. Here's what that sounded like.

Dr. Helen McKibben:

Hello?

Jacob:

Hi Helen. I wanted to have a chat with you about HIPAA compliance and some automation that can make things a little easier.

Dr. Helen McKibben:

Well, I don't know if I have time right now.

Jacob:

Okay. Well, it sounds like right now definitely isn't the time to have this conversation, but if you don't mind me asking, how much time gets taken out of your week on a yearly basis trying to stay HIPAA compliant and do all those processes?

Dr. Helen McKibben:

Actually, that's an excellent question. It's a lot of time.

Jacob:

I've heard that a lot from people like yourself who

have been in this space for so long. It seems to have gotten more and more complicated as the years have gone by. Have you found that to be the case for yourself?

Dr. Helen McKibben:

Yeah. But are you telling me that I could do something about this?

Jacob:

Well, it might be a good fit for you. Most of the organizations I've worked with have to spend a large amount of money to take care of these processes, whether that is bringing somebody on staff or developing a complex internal system. Quite frankly, there've only been a few solutions out there until now. I wanted to see if you are really happy with them. I know you said it already took a lot of time. What are the problems you're facing?

Dr. Helen McKibben:

Yeah. I'm not really happy with the timeframes or the tools we have. I mean, you've got my attention.

Jacob:

Okay. Well, Helen, I know you're busy today. Why don't I do this for you? Are you in front of your computer right now?

Dr. Helen McKibben:

Yes.

Jacob:

If it wouldn't be too much trouble, could you pull up your calendar? I have mine in front of me and maybe we could find a fifteen- to twenty-minute slot next week. I know your hours are valuable, but I think I might be able to save you some time and money.

Dr. Helen McKibben:

I could do that.

Jacob:

Okay. Terrific. How's Thursday at two o'clock sound?

Dr. Helen McKibben:

Excellent.

Jacob:

All right, Helen. Beyond the time you talked about and the cost I mentioned, is there any other headache you're running into with the compliance processes?

Dr. Helen McKibben:

I always have a headache.

Jacob:

Okay. Well, Helen, we're going to take care of you next week here. Please go ahead and accept that calendar invite so I know it didn't get lost in your junk mail, and I'll be prepared with some stuff specifically tailored to healthcare and mental health teams we've worked with before. I'm really excited to connect next week.

Dr. Helen McKibben:

Yeah. Sounds good.

Jacob:

Take care.

Could you see the difference? In that first role-play scenario, I just wanted to get off the phone. I wasn't hearing one thing Jacob was saying, and I wasn't sure he was hearing me either. The second time, when he paused and responded from his experience, he got my attention. I believed that he was listening to who I was and what I was going through, not just sticking to his script to sell me something.

After the scenario, Jacob noted that difficult people often think they know how a conversation is going to go. (And, as I've noted, they expect they'll be able to disrupt you easily.) But once he listened to me say I was short on time and expanded on that idea, I felt listened to and we were able to find common ground.

Dropping after the Fact

The second role-play with Jacob demonstrated what it looks like to use empathy as part of memory retrieval. By *dropping to the blank screen*, Jacob was able to tap into his empathy to connect with me, the "difficult sales prospect", in the moment to turn the conversation around.

But when we're disrupted by others or dealing with difficult people, we don't always catch ourselves in time. Think of a time when this happened to you. You may have responded too quickly or said too much or not enough. When this happens, your brain will continue to bring up the memory of the interaction because the feelings that came with it didn't get resolved.

Here's the good news: As we discussed in Chapter 4, every time you even think about the interaction after it happens, you have another opportunity to *drop to the blank screen*, resolve the feeling, and plan your response for the next time you're in a similar situation. Every time you revisit that feeling, it will light you up physically. When this happens, it's another chance to notice exactly where you're lighting up, *drop to the blank screen* long enough for your brain to configure your point of view, and then make a decision about what you'll say or do differently next time.

If the interaction ever happens again or you feel a similar way around another individual, when you *drop to the blank screen* you'll have a ready-made memory of your decision, and your brain will automatically and unconsciously guide you to implement your plan.

One of my previous interview subjects, J.R., is a town manager. He has plenty of experience with that critical voice that tells him he should have handled something differently. I have been teaching him techniques of *dropping to the blank screen*, even after the fact. Hopefully, our conversation can shed some light on the subject for you.

Dr. Helen McKibben:

Have you ever walked away from an interaction and found yourself constantly second-guessing yourself about it afterwards? "I should have said this" or "I should have done this"?

J.R.:

Consistently. Every two weeks, I run a two-hour public meeting where all the residents of the town can come and voice their grievances or give positive feedback. After each of these meetings, I'm in my head for the next four to six hours straight, going over everything I could have done differently.

Even if it's as small as somebody wanting the road paved when you know you can't afford to do it – you still want to please that person, and you're in your head wondering, "How can I resolve both of these contradictory things at the same time?" I get stuck in a loop, and I lose sleep over it.

Dr. Helen McKibben:

One of the things that I can say in response is that the technique of *drop*, or *drop to the blank screen*, is best done in the moment of being triggered.

Each time you are interacting with a different person in these meetings, I suggest you take the time to notice where you're lighting up, then *drop to the blank screen* until those physically activated areas get back to neutral.

What that will do is start engaging your brain, recalling every time you've dealt with that individual before. It will start your brain in the direction of gathering the information you can use after the meeting to make your decisions. It works best if you do it with one individual—one triggered or disruptive person—at a time.

If you wait until after the meeting or until the next day, you have a number of things your brain hasn't even begun to process. You certainly can *drop* and deal with them afterward, but with so many feelings swimming around up there, it's much harder to isolate and resolve them.

I would like an example of the last time you walked away from an interaction filled with disruption, unable to stop thinking about what they said or did. Could you describe the details of the interaction?

J.R.:

There was a new resident in town, somebody who bought a property just for use in the summer. He came in the winter once and was very upset that the town hadn't plowed his driveway. He came up to me at my personal residence and started to yell at me as soon as he got out of the car. At first, I was kind of taken aback because my previous interactions with this fellow had been very positive.

All I could think at the time was *How do I please this individual? How do I get them to stop yelling at me—to stop trying to disrupt me as much as they are?* It was really unfortunate; if I had handled it better in the moment, I think we could still have had a positive relationship. A couple of weeks later, he came to my residence and threatened to sue me. At that point, I knew I needed to take in the situation before I responded, so I *dropped* and I *dropped* and I *dropped*. I just let him go on and on and on. I didn't say a word. While I was *dropping*, I was able to get a good memory recall of all of the other times that somebody has threatened to sue the town. I was able to *drop* through all of the emotions, and the first words that came into my head were, *Wow. Nobody's threatened to sue the town in three months, I must be doing pretty good.* After he had ended his five-minute rant, all these threats and everything, I just smiled and said, "Okay."

I didn't say anything else.

The memory recall told me that many people have threatened the town before, but none of them have actually sued. This was just going to be another one of those instances. If I had said any more, if I kept trying to please, I would've been digging my own grave. In those types of situations, the best thing to do is to stay silent, say "Okay," and move on.

> After that interaction, I never once tried to figure out what I could have done better. That was the absolute best way I could have treated the situation. If I didn't have that memory recall of all of those times, and I stayed in my head and I tried to please this individual, it would've made things so much worse.

J.R.'s story is a classic example we all can relate to, where an individual expects your first response will be to flip into reading their emotions or pleasing them. All of a sudden you respond in a way they're not accustomed to—by *not* responding right away. They see you shifting and pausing, processing within yourself long enough to identify your point of view. When you do respond, your autonomic nervous system and your voice are stable.

Often people don't listen to *what* we say; they listen to *how* we say it. And the self-assurance that comes with responding from a *blank screen* is far more powerful than the slight (or not-so-slight) hint of desperation in that quick, reactive voice.

> Often people don't listen to what we say; they listen to how we say it.

When you take the time of *dropping to the blank screen*, configuring your experience, and saying your point of view, you completely resolve your triggered feelings—and, just like J.R. did in this example, you protect yourself from the triggered feelings others are trying to project onto you.

What Dropping Does to Another Individual

We've touched on the impact your ability to *drop to the blank screen* can have on the individual who is trying to disrupt you, but let's take a closer look at how that works. J.R. called the update below a "fantastic epilogue" to his story about *dropping to the blank screen*. Here's how he and I talked about it:

J.R.:

> That individual over the last six months has gone on to threaten to sue two other people in town. As soon as he didn't get the response he wanted from me, he moved on to other people.
>
> It's fascinating to see how once you gain this skill you can just see it all happen before you. And you're just able to see the pure ridiculousness of it. What you put up with before was fake and just this person's personality, not a serious issue that needed to be resolved.

Dr. Helen McKibben:

> Let's talk about what happens to the other individual when you *drop to the blank screen*. That timing flips

their feelings and disruptions back to them, and you never know what they're going to do.

Are they going to sit back and start feeling the feelings and offer an apology? Or are they going to run from the very feelings they were trying to transfer to you in the first place, and go find someone else to fill with their disruption?

The wonderful thing about this methodology is that it reeducates the people who knew you in the past as having low self-esteem or trying to please others, showing them that you're not going to do that anymore. They'll eventually move on and/or respect you. We never know which one.

J.R.:

A resident came to my house over the weekend, very upset about a number of things in the town. He was yelling and swearing, and I just let him yell. I maintained eye contact. I didn't say anything. I *dropped to the blank screen* instead. Then, after he was done with his rant, the words came to me: "If you're not going to be respectful, I'm going to have to ask you to leave."

Almost immediately, his whole demeanor changed. It was that second when I didn't respond with anger as he expected that made him respect me enough to have a real conversation. Ever since that moment, we have been friends and colleagues, and we've worked together on a number of issues. If it wasn't for that first interaction, we wouldn't have had that friendship.

Dr. Helen McKibben:

What did you notice after you *dropped to the blank screen*?

J.R.:

It's not just your physical presence that feels different. The whole tone and inflection of your voice will also drop or will change so that you're getting your words out at a much different pace than people are used to. It's a very powerful voice you're speaking with, and it really does make a difference in how people view it. It's so hard to describe, but once you get it, you get it.

If you are flipping into reading and reacting to what other people say right away, they stop listening to you and your response. But if you pause and *drop to that blank screen*, they start to listen. Remember, feel the weight of your legs, the weight of your arms, and the air going into your lungs. Pause long enough to hear your thoughts and respond with your words. They will listen.

The Only Voice to Listen To Is Your Own

It's worth taking a moment here to highlight a very important difference between *dropping to the blank screen* and other methods of interacting with people. Many self-help books and some other therapy approaches would suggest that you remember a particular insight, phrase, or piece of advice when you're triggered to feel. But in reality, when you are being triggered to feel, you don't have enough time (or, often, emotional capacity) to think, *What did that therapist tell me to say?* or *What did that book say I should do right now?*

The reason you are learning this particular method is because, when you're triggered to feel, the brain doesn't retrieve cognition 'til much later, making it all but impossible to recall other third-party voices or insights, no matter how helpful they might be. Think about it for a moment. How many times have you wanted to change the way you respond to people, but in the moment you can't remember what you're supposed to do differently?

When you are triggered, the first thing the brain does is light you up physically. *Dropping to the blank screen* gives you an opportunity to focus inwardly and listen to the brain's configurations for your own response. This method builds total self-reliance because, rather than asking you to remember and regurgitate something someone else told you to say, it only asks you to listen to your own brain. In the moment, it's you—not anyone else—who's equipped to advise you in the best possible way, if you let yourself. You may have to shift and *drop* one, two, three, or four times as you go through all the old feeling memories until you get to the *blank screen*, but once you're there, your brain will generate the best possible ideas to resolve your triggered feelings.

J.R. shares more about his experience managing a small town and using the technique of *dropping to the blank screen.*

J.R.:

A contractor who handles a lot of our road issues came to a meeting one night to throw me off balance so that he could get a better price for a snowplowing contract. He got aggressive as soon as he started to speak. He was looking at me for any sort of cue he could possibly use to bring up another point of attack, but I just *dropped* and *dropped,* letting him keep going the whole time.

I maintained eye contact. I kept looking. I showed him I was listening to what he said, and I could tell he was feeling more and more awkward as he went on because there were no cues for him. Toward the end, he just started to pull things out of the hat. When I finally spoke, all I said was, "Any other public comment?"

When you're able to *drop*, you don't feel the awkwardness and the temptation to jump in just to stop it. It is the other person who begins to feel awkward because their strategy is not working. It really, really just sets you on an even keel, not just when you're dealing with that one person's disruption, but as an example for other people who may be there to cause disruptions themselves.

I don't necessarily worry about the pause being long anymore. I used to be very worried about taking too long to do it, but the longer it goes, the more you're putting back on the person who's trying to trigger you, and the more disruptive it is to them instead of you.

J.R. has come out with several really excellent one-liners in a row, so I want to pause here and remind you again: We aren't advocating that you use J.R.'s responses or telling you what you should say or when you shouldn't say anything. That would require you to remember what some counselor or friend told you to say, rather than focusing on your own perspective. When J.R. is *dropping* in his examples, his decision not to say anything comes from within himself, not some external set of instructions.

Next in our conversation, we discussed how to identify when it *is* time to speak, with me initially answering my own question.

Dr. Helen McKibben:

> How do you know when those words come in? How do you know you've *dropped* long enough?
>
> There isn't a time frame involved here. You just keep *dropping* until eventually you hear certain words and ideas, and then you decide what to say. What's very powerful about this process is that it eventually becomes automatic, replacing the old patterns with a new neuron track configuration for how you deal with or read others.

J.R.:

> I was invited to a meeting with the city that provides ambulance service for my town. We had been in a little conflict over the cost of ambulance services for about six months, and they invited me to a meeting to renegotiate the prices. I got to the meeting ready to go. I'd worked so hard on this, and I just knew we were going to get a reduced rate. So when I realized the

> meeting was actually about raising the rate another 30 percent, I was taken aback.
>
> Everything that I had worked on—everything I'd prepared for the meeting—had been thrown out the window. When I spoke, my words weren't right. I was just in a bad place. So I started to *drop*. I was so disrupted that I knew it would take a while, but I also knew it would be worth it. It wasn't until the very end of the meeting that I was able to respond.
>
> When I did, I was on point.

In this meeting, J.R. had fallen into the trap we talked about in Chapter 1: painting a picture of the outcome ahead of time in order to get around his triggered feelings. We go up in our head, and we put together exactly what we think should happen in that situation. When we get there and it doesn't happen, we have set ourselves up to be devastated, hit with a whole new set of feelings to *drop* through—not to mention the critical voice highlighting everything we just did wrong.

The good news in all of this is that when you react "badly" in a situation with others—and you inevitably will—you now have a method for dealing with those feelings so you're ready to respond effectively the next time.

In conclusion, when we're dealing with disruptive people in any area of our lives, *dropping to the blank screen* lets us listen to our own thoughts, feelings, and ideas, and make decisions about what we need to say or do for ourselves, which resolves the brain from bringing it up over and over again. *Dropping to the blank screen*, replying from our point of view, and then moving on is how we develop and exhibit the high self-esteem (as described in Chapter 2) that indicates to us—and those around us—that we aren't to be messed with.

Chapter 8
Parenting: Influencing Your Child's Self-Esteem

When it comes to applying the methodology of *dropping to the blank screen* to parenting, it helps to talk first about how children learn. During the first two to five years of brain development, children learn primarily by interacting with their parents—mothers, fathers, caregivers, or whoever is raising them during those critical years. The lessons learned and patterns developed by children during this time include how to manage their feelings. As we think about how to support our children in developing healthy coping styles, the first thing we want to do is look at how we, as parents, manage our own feelings.

Remember from Chapter 1 that there are three basic styles of managing feelings:

1. **Immediately getting busy or going up into the head:** This style of managing feelings includes individuals who cannot stop moving physically and/or cognitively—worrying, predicting, thinking, or doing—but who never go through their feelings and resolve them.
2. **Sitting on feelings:** Every time some people are triggered to feel, they bottle it up, letting the avoided feelings build up until they explode into provocation or implode into depression.
3. **Pausing long enough to hear their own point of view:** These individuals never second-guess how they feel or what they hear in themselves. They go through their feelings and make decisions based on what they know and need.

When you look at your style of managing your feelings with challenges involving your children, do you react very quickly, verbally and/or physically? Do you sit on feelings until they build up and you explode or implode? Or do you pause with yourself, listen to what you want to say or do, and respond to your child with what you hear in yourself? Because whatever management style you model for them is the management style they will adopt, too.

With the technique of *dropping to the blank screen*, the goal as a parent is to identify triggered feelings as soon as they happen, go through them and respond thoughtfully and intentionally to resolve each feeling. That is, caregivers want to *drop to the blank screen* before interacting with children.

This method starts out with shifting and noticing where you're lighting up, enabling you to catch yourself and respond appropriately rather than reenacting a style of management you may have learned from your parents during your first five years of development. Yes, sometimes with parenting, you'll find your own parents "coming out of your mouth," unconsciously and automatically. You'll be observing and interacting with your child, and all of a sudden you'll hear a tone of voice that your mother used, or witness yourself doing something your father used to do. *Dropping to the blank screen* gives you a chance to pause and ensure that, if you're sounding like your parents, it's because you actively and thoughtfully chose to do so.

When you do slip up and find yourself falling into old patterns, it is very important for children to realize that they aren't causing our physical reactions.

If your parent comes out of your mouth or you grab your child in a way your parent used to grab you, it is important that you immediately *drop to the blank screen*. Listen to any memory retrieval about how you felt when someone did that with you. Then go back to the child at some point and say, "You know, the other day when I said this . . . " or "The other day when I did this, I didn't mean to, and you didn't do anything wrong. I was reenacting how I was parented, and I'm working on changing it so it doesn't happen with you and me again."

All that being said, please note that one thing we never do is blame our parents for our own shortcomings. Why? Because our parents learned their style of managing feelings or parenting from their parents, who learned from their parents, etc., generation after generation. Blaming your parents only wastes time, distracting you from seeking out more effective styles of parenting that work with your children.

Dropping into Empathy: Feeling Our Children's Feelings

When I spoke with Autumn, a new mother, about the challenges and questions she had about being a parent, the first thing we discussed was a concept called *kinesthetic empathy*. One thing you'll find out about parenting is that if you get triggered by a child's big feelings—and boy, do big feelings get triggered with children—you end up feeling a lot of the feelings and frustrations that they don't know how to express or manage. We call this kinesthetic empathy, and it's a helpful way to understand what children are feeling based on how you end up feeling around them. When you end up filled with your children's feelings, this provides tremendous information on what they're struggling to deal with emotionally.

> When you end up filled with your children's feelings, this provides tremendous information on what they're struggling to deal with emotionally

Let me give you an example. Imagine you're interacting with your child and find yourself filled with anger that wasn't there before. If you *drop to the blank screen*, you can recognize that you're feeling your child's anger, and then go back to your child and empathize. "Oh, I just felt a little angry," you might say. "Are you angry about something?" So you use the emotion to empathize with your child, giving them permission to feel their big feelings while modeling a constructive management strategy.

When a child is overreacting to their own feelings, don't immediately try to stop the feelings because they're triggering your own. Instead, the first thing you want to do is notice that your feelings are active. Notice exactly where those feelings are physically. Ride through them until you're back to neutral before deciding what to say or do with your child. Using that technique, you can help resolve the triggered feelings for both of you, rather than transferring them back to the child to deal with.

If we recognize that our children are experiencing big feelings they may not know what to do with, how do we help them understand and cope with these feelings? That was Autumn's next question, and it led to a fruitful continuation of our discussion about empathy.

Autumn:

What's the best way to talk about emotions with a young child?

Dr. Helen McKibben:

When a child is an infant, they pick up on your tone of voice and tension level. When they're a little older, toddler age, you can add vocabulary. But the best tool when they get older is not advice; it's empathy. So if the child who is a little older is having a hard time in the bathtub, and they don't want to take a bath, you *drop to the blank screen*.

And remember, this isn't a relaxation technique; it's a chance to recall memories. In this case, you may remember how it was for you when you didn't want to take a bath at that age, and you can use those memories to empathize with your child. "I know how it is. I didn't like to take baths either, but it's something we have to do to stay healthy." That way, they'll hear that empathetic response, as opposed to "You'd better," or "You're not going to be able to watch TV tomorrow."

If they hear that frustrated tone of voice, they know how to upset their parents, and they'll do it over and over again. Why? Because they're mean? No, because it's familiar and a way of being in control.

It's so important that parents monitor their own style of managing feelings and are not over – and under-reacting, because that's what the child is going to learn. That's what they're going to hear. That's what they're going to mimic.

When we *drop to the blank screen*, we enable ourselves to be present for our children with empathy.

"I know how it feels to take a bath when you don't want to."

"I know how it feels to have to eat something that's good for you but tastes a little funny."

What the child learns out of that empathy is that there's nothing wrong with them. Their parent has felt that way, too, and their own feelings are perfectly okay.

Dropping into Empathy 2: Sharing Our Feelings with Our Children

If one part of empathy is feeling our children's feelings, the other side of the coin is that we can pass our own feelings onto them, as Autumn and I discussed when she talked about her struggles comforting her child at night.

Autumn:

> My daughter is eleven months old, and we have to deal with a lot of crying and the lack of sleep that comes with being a new parent. I sometimes find myself picking her up at 3:00 a.m., just out of sheer exhaustion, and even then, it doesn't comfort her. Is there something I could be doing, even at this early age, to start incorporating better techniques?

Dr. Helen McKibben:

Simple. When you're frustrated, be sure you are *dropped to the blank screen* before you pick up your child. Because children feel our tensions, they'll feel if your neuromuscular system is heightened—you're frustrated—or if it's released and *dropped to the blank screen*—you're calm. You want to be sure in any physical interaction with them that you're operating from the *blank screen* when you touch them.

Autumn:

That makes a lot of sense. And I definitely do notice that. If I'm tense trying to rock her, it doesn't help.

Your child will pick up when you're frustrated, and they'll cue off of that. When you can feel your own tension heightening, be sure you are *dropping to the blank screen* before you interact with them. You want your child to be interacting with you after you've fully resolved the physiological changes that go with triggered feelings.

As a side note, *dropping to the blank screen* can be beneficial during breastfeeding, too. If you are having trouble breastfeeding, and you're worried about it—*Oh my milk won't come in* or *What's wrong?*—that's not going to help. But if you *drop to the blank screen*, you'll resolve those feelings and your brain will get enough oxygen and blood flow to respond in the moment, physiologically, to giving that child milk. It will start to flow with abundance.

Helping Children Develop High Self-Esteem

High self-esteem is formed when a child in their early years of development has a feeling-reaction, a read of a situation, or an idea of something they really wanted to do. In the child's learning, there are two types of parenting responses about a child's feelings and ideas, and it's the one that comes with *dropping* that helps them develop that high self-esteem we all desire for our children.

So, when faced with a child's big feelings or ideas, the parent should pause, *drop*, and respond non-reactively and with reinforcement. For example:

"Oh, that's an interesting idea."

"Yes, I've felt that way before."

"Hmm, what do you think?"

These responses reinforce a child's connection to their feelings and help cultivate high self-esteem. In Chapter 2, I shared several examples of the types of responses that harm a child's developing sense of self-reliance, and I encourage you to go back to that chapter and review them. These are the responses that teach a child that their feelings are invalid or that their ideas either aren't worth exploring or are too big to explore independently. Rather than developing the child's confidence, these responses teach them to second-guess their own perspectives and abilities. In Chapter 2, and throughout the book, we've seen the trouble that can lead children into as they grow up.

> The best way to help children develop high self-esteem is to teach them to listen to their first feelings, thoughts, or ideas by enforcing them through empathy

The best way to help children develop high self-esteem is to teach them to listen to their first feelings, thoughts, or ideas by enforcing them through empathy. Believe it or not, with hard work, this is possible at *any* stage of a child's development. Even, as I coached Autumn, the dreaded "terrible twos."

Autumn:

> What about the terrible twos? Having an infant is hard enough. I have friends who have two-year-olds, and it looks even harder. How do you keep a cool

head when dealing with someone who just doesn't have reason yet?

Dr. Helen McKibben:

You keep a cool body first, and your head will follow. Let me give you an example. Let's say you're in a grocery store and you've got a child who's picking everything off the shelves, asserting independence, and trying to be in control. After all, that's what the terrible twos are about. The parents who make it out of that grocery store in one piece are the parents who don't overreact. They're the ones who can *drop* and make different decisions about what to say or do in that moment.

Whatever they hear in themselves, they have to trust, whether it's leaving the store or being firm (but calm and measured) with the child. Instead of a high-pitched "Dear God, please stop that! You're driving Mommy nuts," it's a simple, assertive "No, we're not getting cereal today." Instead of a panicky "We can't stay here if you keep acting like this!", it's a calm "We'll have to move to a different location."

Again, the terrible-twos child is listening to the immediacy of the parents' response and determining whether they can get their parents to change their mind. So if you use *dropping to the blank screen*, stay firm and consistent, and keep your voice calm and neutral, they will know that they cannot knock you off balance, and they'll be far more likely to stop trying.

The other thing I reminded Autumn about the terrible twos is that it is a very emotional time. Children are beginning to feel a lot of feelings, and they've got limited language—like the word 'No'—to go with it. At this stage, they are watching every move you make and observing how you manage your own feelings to learn how to regulate their own emotions.

No matter how tempting it may be, your success in surviving that trip to the grocery store—and modeling feelings management for your little one—isn't going to come from yelling and being tense, or fuming silently until you explode in the car after leaving the store. Instead, it's going to come from pausing, listening to yourself, and going through your emotions, then responding intentionally based on the feedback your brain provides.

Dropping with Older Children

As noted, the early years of childhood from two to five are very formative. But what if your child is older than five—if they're past this formative age range—and you're either just getting started on this work or still perfecting your techniques? Good news—as I reassured Autumn, you're not too late!

Autumn:

You spoke a little bit about how children learn and how crucial these early years are. Does that mean that their learning styles and development are set in stone after age five?

Dr. Helen McKibben:

Absolutely not. Children learn by what we do, so the lovely thing about the methodology of using the *blank screen* is that, if you work on yourself and adopt that healthy style of managing feelings, no matter what ages your children are, they will adapt with you at almost any age. If you're pausing, *dropping into the blank screen,* and then responding in your interactions with children, they will learn to do the same.

No matter the child's age, it is very important that the parents learn to monitor their own style of managing feelings and set a healthy example for the child.

Bringing Dropping *to Life*

To illustrate how all these concepts might play out in a difficult interaction with a child, let's look at how Autumn and I explored using empathy to connect with her toddler during bath time.

Autumn:

> My daughter is pretty young, so we haven't crossed this threshold too much yet, but when I was five or six, I hated taking a bath. My parents really had to beg and cajole me. And we had a little star chart, and Mom would put a star on the chart for every day that I took a bath.

Dr. Helen McKibben:

> Could you give me the dialogue back and forth between you and the parent?

Autumn:

> "It's bath time."
> "No, I got a bath yesterday."
> "Well, you need to get one every day."
> "No, I don't want to get a bath."
> "Well, you have two stars this week already. Don't you want a third star?"

"No, I don't want to get a star. I don't want to take a bath."

That sort of thing.

Dr. Helen McKibben:

That's a great example. We're going to reverse this. I'm going to be the child and you're going to be the parent.

Autumn:

Okay.

Dr. Helen McKibben:

The first time, I want you to respond the way you're talking about as I'm fighting you to take a bath. And then the second time, we're going to add the *drop to the blank screen*. Let's see how this works.

Autumn:

All right. It's time to take a bath.

Dr. Helen McKibben:

No, I don't want to take a bath. I took a bath yesterday.

Autumn:

Well, you're filthy today. You need to take a bath.

Dr. Helen McKibben:

I'm not filthy. What do you mean? I'm fine. You just washed my hair yesterday.

Autumn:

Look at all the chocolate all over your face. Get in the bathtub.

Dr. Helen McKibben:

I'll just wipe it off. I'm fine. I just want to go to bed.

Autumn:

Come on. I'm going to count to three. One, two, three.

Dr. Helen McKibben:

No three, no three.

Autumn:

Get in the bathtub now.

Dr. Helen McKibben:

No, I don't want to. I'm not going to take a bath.

Autumn:

I'm going to call Daddy.

Dr. Helen McKibben:
> Cut.

Next, we used an iteration in which I asked Autumn to *drop to the blank screen* until she was back in neutral and able to respond from her own perspective, from a place of empathy, rather than just reacting to her child.

Dr. Helen McKibben:
> I don't want to take a bath. I took a bath yesterday. Mommy, mommy, did you hear me? I don't want to take a bath.

Autumn:
> You need to take a bath every day.

Dr. Helen McKibben:
> Well, what about the ... where's my ducky? I don't see my ducky. Did you do something with my ducky? If you want me to take a bath, I have to have the ducky.

Autumn:
> Taking a bath can be fun.

Dr. Helen McKibben:

Oh, well, maybe when you were a kid, but I don't like taking a bath at all. What were you like when you were a kid? Did you like taking baths?

Autumn:

I didn't like being told what to do.

Dr. Helen McKibben:

Oh, me too. I know how that is. So, hey, that's great. I don't like to be told what to do either. Isn't that amazing? You're like me.

Autumn:

We are more alike than you know.

Dr. Helen McKibben:

Cut.

Did you hear the change in your tone of voice? It flipped the child. First, she diverted the subject, changed it and it didn't work, and she ended up empathizing with her mother. You see the difference?

Autumn:

Yeah.

Dr. Helen McKibben:

When we were doing this, did you think the *dropping* took too long?

Autumn:

A little bit, like when you said, "Mommy, Mommy, didn't you hear me?" I know kids often need that immediate validation, and it was tempting to respond immediately. But I was trying really hard not to.

Dr. Helen McKibben:

Do you want to reverse roles to see what the pause feels like?

Autumn:

Yeah. Yeah.

Dr. Helen McKibben:

So why don't we do that? I'll be the parent, you're the child. First time, I'm not going to *drop to the blank screen*. The second time, I am.

Autumn:

But I don't want to take a bath.

Dr. Helen McKibben:

But you have to take a bath, it's Sunday.

Autumn:

But I took a bath yesterday.

Dr. Helen McKibben:

Yeah, but we always take baths on Sunday, it's the odd day of the week.

Autumn:

Heather's mommy doesn't make her take a bath.

Dr. Helen McKibben:

I'm not Heather's mommy, I'm your mommy. And I'm saying you have to take a bath.

Autumn:

Well, I don't like you.

Dr. Helen McKibben:

Well, that's OK because you still have to take a bath. Cut.

This time I'm going to *drop to the blank screen* before I respond. And when I respond, I'm going to respond with what I hear in myself.

Autumn:

Why do I have to take a bath? I don't want to take a bath.

Dr. Helen McKibben:

It's Sunday.

Autumn:

I don't want to have to take a bath every Sunday. It's not fair.

Did you hear me?

I'm not taking a bath. I'm not taking a bath. You can't make me.

Dr. Helen McKibben:

When I was little, I didn't like taking baths either, but you have to.

Autumn:

I don't believe you were ever little like me.

Dr. Helen McKibben:

Oh, I remember how it felt. I didn't like not being in control.

Autumn:

>I kind of don't know how to respond to that.
>
>Well, I don't like baths, and I don't like you.

Dr. Helen McKibben:

>I used to get mad at my mother too.
>
>Cut.
>
>So let me ask you a question. How did it feel the first time? How did it feel the second time, being the child when I *dropped to the blank screen*?

Autumn:

>I definitely felt like the "I don't like you" line ... I felt your frustration the first time around. You just didn't have a response. And I felt power with that line because it threw you.

Dr. Helen McKibben:

>All my physical reactions are what you were watching.

Autumn:

>Yeah. And then the second time around, I didn't get that at all. And in fact, I got empathy back, and I wasn't expecting that as a child.

Dr. Helen McKibben:
> So, what do children read? What you say or how you say it? They read *how* you say or do things, not the words themselves. That's how they learn.

During that role-play, Autumn was able to retrieve her memories and empathize by *dropping to the blank screen*. You may have learned to *drop to the blank screen* in a sitting position, but obviously, with children, you are going to notice you're triggered when you're sitting, standing, walking, driving, or lying down. No matter what position you find yourself in, work on *dropping* long enough to listen to your words and point of view. When you're ready, decide what to say or do for yourself.

Whether your children are two weeks, two years, or even twenty years old, modeling this behavior will help them develop the high self-esteem they need to listen to and trust themselves first, saving them a world of anxiety and hang-ups as they grow.

Chapter 9
Dating in Neutral: How to Change Who You Attract

This chapter is all about dating in "neutral", one of the terms used to describe being at the *blank screen*. Being in neutral means listening to your own thoughts, feelings, and ideas as the brain has configured them. When you're dating in neutral, you're committing to using the *drop to the blank screen* method every time you're triggered to feel by an interaction with a person you're dating (or considering dating) or a romantic situation. When you do this, you reach a position where your physiology is at neutral, your emotions are at neutral, and you're making good decisions for yourself. You're not reacting. You are stable, and people will sense that about you. When you're at neutral, you can't be knocked off balance.

Think about your dating life now. What kind of individuals do you attract? Are they the kind of individuals you'd like to be attracting? Why do you think you keep attracting the same kinds of people? In this chapter, we'll look at how the technique of *dropping to the blank screen* influences who you attract and how you interact with people you're dating.

Remember that the brain's first response to triggered feelings is to light us up physically. This might include sweating, an elevated heart rate, holding our breath, or tensing our muscles. Your response will be unique, but once you know what response to look for, you'll discover that a physical reaction occurs every time you're triggered to feel. My goal in this book has been to teach you to go through those triggered feelings so you can listen to yourself before you respond to other people. You've already seen the impact that can have on your own confidence and others' perceptions of you, and that power extends to romantic relationships, too. In the context of dating, this technique has the power to change the type of people you attract and the way you relate to them.

You can change the neural connections in your brain by simple methodologies that redo the patterns developed during childhood, empowering you to take actions that reverse the default choices made during dating interactions. Doing this involves leveraging the memory recall accessed by *dropping to the blank screen* so that the brain reconfigures all the times you've felt a certain way before, either positive or negative. This helps in making decisions based on your own perspective and experiences.

Who Are You Attracted To?

Before we get to what *dropping* looks like in this context, let's examine how our attraction patterns—who we're typically drawn to and who's typically drawn to us—come about. These patterns, like so much else about the way we interact with the world, are set in the first five years of brain development. The reason the first five years have such a strong influence is because our brains are designed to be attracted to what is familiar, not necessarily what's good or bad for us. It is during those five years that familiarity is established through the way we experience our caregivers interacting with us and each other. You or I could walk into a room of five hundred people, and we would each find ourselves attracted to different people—most likely the people who are similar to our parents.

How Does Your Date Manage Feelings?

One of the key characteristics we subconsciously look for in others is a familiar style of managing feelings. So, when you find yourself attracted to someone, it's very likely that their style mirrors your parents'. Remember that there are basically three styles of managing feelings when people are triggered to feel. The first style is to distract ourselves by getting busy physically or cognitively. The second style is to sit on the feelings until we explode or implode. The third style is to pause, listen to our own point of view, and make a confident decision. If you are on a date with someone who is exhibiting a Number One or Number Two style, you will end up filled with the feelings that they're not dealing with.

How can you identify a potential partner's style of managing feelings? You might detect that a date uses the first style if they can't allow for there to be any silences. They talk over everything else that is being said, they're in constant motion, or they don't allow pauses. Another indicator may be that, once they meet you, they can't stop texting you. After the first date, they're blowing up your phone.

A date who uses the second style shuts down anytime a feeling is triggered. Every time they're triggered to feel, they say, "Oh, I'm fine. No problem. Oh, your comment didn't bother me." They just sit there. But when the date is over, they never call again because they were so upset even though they didn't address that emotion. If the relationship progresses past that first date, the silent stewing continues, with very little open and honest communication, until experiencing just one more triggered feeling could cause the individual to explode or implode.

When you identify these patterns in the people you're dating, you have to be able to detect whether you're uncomfortable. If you are, that would indicate your date has transferred their unprocessed feelings to you, compromising your own ability to stay neutral and make confident, level decisions. That's the danger of dating people who are disconnected from their feelings, and why you want to protect yourself by being *dropped* around your dates. You don't want them to disrupt you (or see that they can disrupt you) with the feelings they're running from.

Consider this scenario: A young woman is on a date, and every time the waiter approaches the table, her companion barks at them for one reason or another. "You're not bringing our food on time," or "This place is lousy," or "Refill my water." He's exhibiting either a Number One style of running from his feelings by reacting right away, or a Number Two style of sitting on feelings 'til they build up. If the latter, he's probably been sitting on feelings for a while already, and what the young woman is witnessing is the explosion, triggered by the poor waiter not doing something perfectly.

It would be easy for this young woman to get caught up in her date's attitude, either agreeing with him or obsessing over "fixing" feelings. Instead, she should *drop to the blank screen* to retrieve memories that will help her notice how she ended up around such a rude and aggressive person and how similar situations in her past have impacted her. Then she can make a decision about whether she wants to feel that way again—and whether the date should continue.

Someone may also observe the third style of managing feelings on a date. Consider the same restaurant, the same young woman, and a date who knows how to manage his feelings effectively. This individual is triggered by that lethal combination of hunger and slow service. However, instead of reacting impulsively, he pauses and goes through his feelings. He knows he is agitated, but he sits back, *dropping to the blank screen* until he can decide what to say to the waiter.

When he finally responds to the situation, it's to respectfully flag down the waiter and kindly ask, "Could you please help us out in getting our meal?"

Dropping into First Impressions

When you meet other people, you want to be able to use your first gut reaction—formed by your emotional intelligence and instincts—to read the other individual. In particular, you want to notice how you end up feeling around them. That is the most important thing. If they're running from feelings, the probability is very high that you'll end up "catching" the disrupted feelings they're not dealing with.

For this reason, online dating can be tricky, and you will want to meet potential prospects in person as soon as possible. Limiting your exchanges to online chats or text messages can make it difficult to effectively assess how an individual leaves you feeling. Sports clubs, recreation classes, and meet-up events make it much easier to assess the people you're meeting. They also tend to bring out more promising candidates, because you're starting with common interests and, usually, shared geography. As a bonus, you can already assume the people you're meeting have some level of positive self-esteem, because they're selecting activities based on what they know about themselves and their own likes and dislikes.

No matter how you meet people, though, your priority in forming your first impression should be listening to your initial emotional reactions upon interacting with them. Notably, you're looking for your interpretation of whether the person you're dating has high or low self-esteem. We covered self-esteem in depth in Chapter 2, but as a refresher: People with high self-esteem respond to people who pause, listen to themselves, and know their point of view. Someone with high self-esteem is attractive because they know their own thoughts, feelings, and ideas, and they understand what they want in their life. Low self-esteem, on the other hand, is when an individual doesn't know themselves well enough to listen to their own perspectives and instead flips into reading the other person. These people want to be taken care of, to be appeased, and for their partners to do all the work in the dating process.

> Someone with high self-esteem is attractive because they know their own thoughts, feelings, and ideas, and they understand what they want in their life

So how do you identify whether a potential partner has high or low self-esteem? This requires developing the ability to pause and listen to yourself or the words your brain puts together as you interact with other individuals. That time allows for you to sense your gut instinct. It's called emotional intelligence. You access it by *dropping to the blank screen* long enough to hear your point of view.

Imagine that you have gone out on a date. The date was all right, but you can't say you're all that excited about the individual. In the next week, though, they're texting you five times a day, practically begging for a response. This should cue you that something is unbalanced with the other individual—something has triggered them, and they're running from feelings (in Number One style) by texting you. You may feel panicky, frustrated, or anything in between by this persistence. But it's very important that you don't respond until you *drop to the blank screen* long enough to go through whatever you're feeling and hear your point of view. Once you've done that, you can respond with honesty instead of trying to please or appease them. An honest, measured response will flip their disrupted feelings back to them, and they'll realize that they can't manipulate you like that. They may continue to text you, but more likely than not, your self-esteem-based response will either inspire a change in behavior or free you both up to move on.

When it comes to meeting and dating people for the first time—and forming those all-important first impressions—there is a set of things you want to look for in yourself. To identify how you feel around a date—and whether they're someone with high self-esteem who could make a healthy match—start by asking yourself these questions:

> Does this person rub me the wrong way?
> Did I walk away from the date saying, "I wouldn't want to spend any time with this person"?
> Did I meet their friends?
> Did their friends rub me the wrong way?
> Could I be friends with this person, given who they are and how I end up feeling around them?

If your first impression is that you couldn't be friends with a person, that's a sign that you shouldn't continue to date them. In the very beginning of dating, when you're just meeting somebody, your instincts may be telling you, *I don't want to hang around with this person. I don't want to be friends with them.* Listen to yourself.

If the early indicators aren't quite so clear, move on to this next set of questions:

- Did I end up with emotions that weren't there before I interacted with them? (In other words, did I end up with their feelings instead of staying with my own?)
- Did I end up with sexual feelings that weren't there before I interacted with them? (In other words, could I have been manipulated into feeling their feelings instead of staying with my own?)

Why are these questions important? If you remain in neutral during the date and don't end up letting yourself be disrupted, there's a good chance that both of you are healthy. You feel connected. But if you do end up feeling disrupted and filled with manipulative feelings that weren't there before, the individual that you are going on the date with may be running from their own feelings and issues.

If so, the other person gets a sense of control by projecting those disruptions onto you or by getting you to do what they (think they) want, instead of noticing and going through their own feelings. This is a manipulation technique that gives people with low self-esteem a temporary sense of control. If you leave a date thinking, *How did I end up with these feelings? They aren't even mine*, that's an important indicator that you should *drop* and figure out what feelings you've picked up from someone else versus how *you* felt on the date. Finally, ask yourself the next two questions, which follow the same line of thinking:

> Did my date allow me to pause or *drop* until I found my own words or preferences, or did they immediately try to talk me into what *they* wanted?
> What style of managing their feelings did they show?

Any red flags you pick up on as you ask yourself these questions—and *really listen* to the answers—are indicators that your date had low self-esteem and likely wasn't a good fit for you.

Low Self-Esteem in Action

To bring the concept of identifying low self-esteem to life in another way, let's look at an example of someone whose low self-esteem prohibits them from even allowing you to state your point of view. When you start to pause and *drop*, this person cannot tolerate the silence. They will immediately speak over you, urge you to respond quickly, or try to talk you into their own point of view instead of waiting to hear yours. This tendency will give you a preview of what it would be like dating this person in the future. Here's the scenario:

As the waiter clears the plates from the table, your date says, "Hey, do you want to come to my apartment?"

You say, "It's only the first date."

"Ah, you know you want to come to my apartment," he replies. He's testing you to see if he can talk you out of your point of view. This is an indicator that your date is trying to control you in order to cope with his own self-esteem.

If you try to please him by giving in, he'll read that you have low self-esteem as well, and the pattern of manipulation and compromise will continue. But if you stick with your point of view, saying, "Nope, I don't do that on first dates," he'll see your high self-esteem and know you can't be manipulated. Sure, there's a risk that he'll go on and date someone else that he *can* manipulate, but if he can't handle your self-esteem, is he really a good fit anyway?

If you're on a date and someone is acting badly or in a way that upsets you, it's more than likely an attempt (perhaps subconsciously) to see if you'll jump in and try to fix them or compromise your own experience to make the date work anyway. Here's what you have to remember: People interact with us the way they learn to interact with others growing up. You are not causing their behavior, and you can't fix it, no matter how accommodating you are.

If you'd brought your own low self-esteem to this date, you'd likely forget that you are not causing their behavior, and you would flip into trying to smooth things over. But if you showed up with high self-esteem, you would shift, pause, *drop* to listen to your point of view, and make a decision about future dates accordingly.

Practicing the *dropping* technique and learning to date in neutral is the best way to rewire your attraction patterns and stop yourself from being drawn to people who aren't right for you. Why? Mostly because *dropping* helps you build your own high self-esteem so you're no longer tempted to compromise your own feelings and perspectives. People with low self-esteem attract others with low self-esteem, and vice versa.

> Learning to date in neutral is the best way to rewire your attraction patterns and stop yourself from being drawn to people who aren't right for you

Now that we've covered how to identify low self-esteem in others, we'll look in the next section at how to show up differently yourself to make better dating decisions.

Showing Up with High Self-Esteem

People test us all the time on first dates, looking to see how easily they can maintain the upper hand. For example, imagine a fellow asks you on a date and you suggest an Italian restaurant you love. He agrees. Then, ten minutes before you're supposed to meet, he calls and says, "Hey, I want to go to a Chinese restaurant instead."

Your default reaction, born from low self-esteem, might be to bend over backward to get across town to the new restaurant on time. But the individual with high self-esteem would pause long enough to notice how she feels about the change—and his last-minute timing. Then she will make a decision based on what she heard in herself, which might be "That's fine, but given the late notice, I'll be about forty-five minutes late," or even "I had my heart set on Italian and I'm already on the way to the restaurant. Let me know if you still want to meet me there or if you'd rather reschedule."

This measured response, enabled by *dropping to the blank screen*, flips the disruption back to the individual who is testing his date. When he learns she's not easily manipulated, it's up to him to decide whether he's mature enough to date someone with high self-esteem or whether he'd rather move on to an "easier target".

My job is to teach you a method to become present with high self-esteem, like the woman in this example. Why? Because in dating, being present in this way naturally filters out individuals who have low self-esteem, and attracts people who have high self-esteem. How do you do this? You practice the concept of *dropping to the blank screen* using the steps described in the Introduction of this book.

Dropping accomplishes three things in dating. First, your date will read that you know yourself and can't be talked out of your point of view. The method also flips people's disruptive dating behavior back to them. If they don't want to do their own work to respond from their own feelings, they might move on and date someone else. Third, and perhaps most importantly, *dropping to the blank screen* after you are triggered to feel while on a date will help you listen to your point of view and respond with high self-esteem. Remember: high self-esteem attracts high self-esteem.

I spoke to J.R. about his experiences in dating, and he shared a wonderful example of showing up with high self-esteem to what turned out to be a difficult date.

J.R.:

I was invited to a New Year's party by a wonderful young woman who was a nerd like me. She was throwing a *Harry Potter*-themed party and invited me to come as her date. I picked out a costume for it and went all out because she was really excited about it.

When I got there, she was dressed up as a character, too, and she had prepared all sorts of *Harry Potter*-themed food and drinks. She had obviously put a lot of effort into it. But as the other guests started to come in, I realized that we were the only people in costumes. The others weren't necessarily appreciating or understanding the amount of work she had put into the party.

As the night progressed, she seemed to be fine, and we had some great conversations. But then, right at the end of the night, when getting ready to count down to midnight, I asked for a virgin drink, and she just blew up at me, calling me *sexist* for using that term. I was really taken aback because I know I didn't do anything to warrant how upset she'd gotten. So I just counted down to midnight and then ordered an Uber home. I was not going to put myself in a position to be treated that way again.

Dr. Helen McKibben:

Are you saying you didn't scramble to fix the situation?

J.R.:

There was nothing to fix. I hadn't done anything wrong. She had put all this effort into this party, and I was the only person who'd really appreciated it. And yet she took out all her frustrations on me at the end of the night. It was really no fun. She was a wonderful person, but if that's how she managed her feelings, I couldn't date her. I was never going to allow that to happen again.

J.R. recognized that his date was likely managing her triggered feelings in the way that she'd learn to do so growing up—in her case, by sitting on them till they built up and exploded. She was using the Number Two style of feelings management, but J.R. managed to use the healthier Number Three style. He paused and went through those very difficult feelings physically, then listened to his thoughts and made a decision to go home. If J.R. had had low self-esteem, he might have gone up into his head, spinning, looking for ways to fix her and the situation. He would have missed an opportunity to use his own feelings in his decision-making. Rather than taking on his date's emotions, J.R. *dropped to the blank screen* and used the way he felt to make decisions for himself.

How can you show up on dates with the same level of self-esteem J.R. displayed at the party?

Be sure that you *drop to the blank screen* before you arrive. Be sure that, if you are interacting by phone or text, you *drop to the blank screen* before every response. Why so frequently? It's just like how we deal with the fear of flying. One *drop* doesn't resolve the fear of flying all at once; rather, every time you even think about flying, you have to *drop to the blank screen*. Each time, your fear and anxiety are reduced to a more manageable size, and by the time the captain turns on the seat belt sign, you have only a small level of feelings to *drop* through, because you've dealt with this before.

The same is true in dating. If you're anticipating a date, you don't want to arrive anxious. Every time you even think about the date or the individual, *drop to the blank screen*. Do it again when you're trying to figure out the perfect outfit to wear, and when you're in the shower or putting on your makeup. *Drop* as you're walking to the restaurant and when you sit in your chair. *Drop to the blank screen* before you say a word.

When you've done this work ahead of time, your anxiety won't be showing when you speak. You'll be solid in that chair, already *dropped* and full of self-esteem. If you're triggered at any point on the date, guess what? You won't have to *drop* far to get back to neutral.

Remember that people read your presentation. They don't listen to what you say, for example, nearly as much as how you say it. If you *drop* and then say what *you* want based on the information you retrieve—not based on what you think your date wants to hear—your date will read your stability. They will read that you have high self-esteem and won't be easy to manipulate.

As you continue to get to know someone, and you're interacting back and forth, check in with yourself to be sure you're still responding from neutral instead of reacting from anxiety or fear.

> Are you pausing with each of the emails, text messages, or verbalizations back and forth?
>
> Are you sitting long enough to hear your point of view before responding?

Pausing will demonstrate your high self-esteem, empowering you to attract those who also bring high self-esteem to the table and who are actually interested in *you* and *your* point of view—not just what you can do for them.

People Pleasing in Relationships

In opposition to J.R.'s self-determined, confident decision at the New Year's Eve party, someone with low self-esteem will flip into reading other people and trying to fix their own feelings by fixing the other person's. That is the definition of people-pleasing. A people-pleaser responds to the other person's triggered feelings by looking to them to guide their decisions, instead of learning to pause and listen to themselves. These individuals have shut out their own feelings in service of fixing other people or situations.

Some of the things we would say about an individual who's people-pleasing or reading others in the dating process is that they do things specifically to try to keep the other person happy. For example, they will communicate excessively with the individual at the expense of their own friendships. At the core of this kind of people-pleasing is that these individuals are attempting to take on responsibility for the feelings another person isn't dealing with at all.

What happens, sadly, is that those unfelt and unnoticed feelings transfer to the people-pleaser, leaving them filled with disruption. Later on, they think, *How did I end up feeling this way?* That's because what they are feeling isn't theirs; rather, it is transferred from the person who wasn't dealing with her own feelings.

When you notice that someone's feelings are transferring to you, this is your cue to immediately stop. Shift to notice where you're lit up, then *drop to the blank screen* long enough for your brain to configure memories of every time you've felt this way with this individual or others. As you know, the brain is brilliant at memory retrieval, and it will spit out simple ideas for preventing this disruption, now and in the future. If you're still in the situation, you will then decide how to respond in the moment. If you're ruminating on something that happened previously, you'll decide what to do differently in your next interaction.

Andrew and I talked about his experience with people pleasing—or the temptation to be a people-pleaser—in dating.

Dr. Helen McKibben:

So, Andrew, have you ever been in a situation where you're dating someone and you ended up disrupted? And then you couldn't stop thinking about it afterward?

Andrew:

Yeah, absolutely. Whenever I have a significant other, I spend a lot of time with them. And for me, the time apart is usually filled with texting. With one partner, there were several times where I would put a lot of effort and planning into hanging out with friends I hadn't seen in a really long time. When I did, and when I wasn't available to respond to text messages quickly, it became, "Why aren't you texting me back every five minutes?"

This really took away from the time I had with my friends, and it wasn't just that I would look back and retrospectively realize I'd had a bad time or that my partner's anger wasn't worth the time with my friends. But even in the moment, my friends would ask me,

"Are you okay? What are you doing?" I was on my phone instead of with them, and that was definitely a big point of disruption for me.

Whenever you bring a significant other into your life, you have to balance them and your existing friends. And when you have friends they don't like or don't approve of, or if they give you a really bad time or have a bad attitude when you're hanging out with your friends, I think that's one of the things that makes you second-guess yourself the most. "I know this person. They're my friend. Why would I want to not be friends with them anymore because of your influence?" That definitely made me have a lot of resentment for this partner—that she was asking me to choose between pleasing her or spending quality time with my friends.

Dating is especially complicated with so many communication platforms. It's easy for us to expect immediate responses or always-open lines of connection with our partners, when in reality that immediate response isn't as important as the feelings and the emotion behind it.

But still, to show the other person you care about them, you're willing to do more in terms of communicating and sacrificing things. And it comes to a point where they expect that level of attention as

> standard operating procedure. It's really a lot of work on yourself, and might not be a fair trade-off.
>
> I think one of the biggest patterns I've noticed in some of my relationship turmoil is that moment when I stop doing things because I want to make my significant others happy, and instead I start doing things to avoid making them upset with me. At first, it seems like a very small caveat. But by the end of it, you can end up with an anxiety that's not even yours.

Andrew's observation that people will know if they can fill you with their anxiety and get you to do what they want is right on point. To help him see the value of pausing, going through his own emotions, and listening and using those emotions to make decisions about how to respond—instead of just trying to please or fix other people—we explored a role-play scenario.

In the first round below, I asked him to respond the way he did in the interaction with the individual he was dating.

Dr. Helen McKibben:

> So why didn't you text me immediately?

Andrew:

Oh, I was finishing up work.

Dr. Helen McKibben:

Well, I don't believe you.

Andrew:

I mean, I was at work. I'm there every day. What do you mean?

Dr. Helen McKibben:

Well, I don't know if I can trust you. I mean, if you don't text me, I don't know what else you're doing.

Andrew:

I mean, I'm working, right?

Before the second iteration of our role-play scenario, I walked Andrew through the steps of *dropping to the blank screen*. For the next interaction, I asked him to shift and notice exactly where he was lighting up every time I said something that triggered a feeling. I asked him to *drop to the blank screen* long enough for those physical areas to go back to neutral and to respond to me only after he was at the *blank screen* and could answer based on what he heard in himself, not reacting to what I was saying. See if you can tell the difference.

Dr. Helen McKibben:
Well, why didn't you text me immediately?

Andrew:
I have a lot on my plate.

Dr. Helen McKibben:
Well, so do I, and I just can't stand worrying and thinking about you. You should be wanting to fix my feelings by texting me back.

Andrew:
I don't know if I should be fixing your feelings.

Dr. Helen McKibben:
Of course you should. You're my partner. I mean, if I don't feel good, then I don't do well in school or in sports. Of course you want to fix my feelings.

Andrew:
I definitely want to be there for you, but I don't know how much control I have over your feelings.

Andrew could feel the difference between his emotions and responses from the first interaction to the second. Next, we reversed the role-play so he could feel what *dropping to the blank screen* (or not) does to the person who's being manipulative.

This first scene, while I was role-playing as Andrew, I responded the way I had heard him responding to her before *dropping*.

Andrew (as his partner):

Why didn't you text me immediately after you were done?

Dr. Helen McKibben:

You know I always text you. I guess I was busy. I was just wrapping things up.

Andrew:

Well, you didn't text me this time. I don't even know if I can trust you. What were you doing?

Dr. Helen McKibben:

I don't remember what I was doing. It was something for school.

Andrew:

Well, I just really don't believe you. You haven't been there for me recently, and I just . . . I don't know. I don't know.

Dr. Helen McKibben:

What can I do to fix this?

We cut the scene and then started again, with Andrew playing his partner. This time, though, I took the time to notice where I was lighting up, *dropped to the blank screen* long enough to hear my point of view, and then responded with what I heard in myself after I got to the *blank screen*.

Andrew:

Why didn't you text me immediately when you were done?

Dr. Helen McKibben:

This sounds so familiar.

Andrew:

Well, yeah, you never text me anymore. I never know what you're doing.

Dr. Helen McKibben:
I love you, and this makes me so sad.

Andrew:
It makes me sad when you don't text me back right away. I have no idea what you're doing.

Dr. Helen McKibben:
I'm very hungry. Would you like to join me for a sandwich?

Andrew:
I don't know. Not really. I don't know why you wouldn't have texted me back and now you want to go get food?

When we finished, I asked Andrew how he felt (as his partner) in each of the scenarios. In the first, he said he felt in control, as it was so easy for him to get me to react to his own emotions. The second time, though, when I *dropped* before responding, he felt no sense of control. Instead, he said he found himself frustrated that I wouldn't react the way he wanted me to.

In that second scenario, Andrew was experiencing exactly the phenomenon I've been telling you about. He was trying to disrupt me rather than dealing with his emotions, but instead, I flipped those emotions right back to him. Instead of feeling in control of me, he ended up having to deal with his own emotions.

In that situation, you also give the would-be manipulator an opportunity to think through or look carefully at what they're doing. If they're capable of that, they'll either turn around and give you an apology or be able to talk about what's happening internally. If they *can't* take that step back, well, you have more information about whether or not they're a fitting romantic partner.

Money Talks. Drop to Listen

Disagreements about money can almost always be used to illustrate relationship problems, starting from the very first date. The way money is handled early on sets up patterns, preferences, or very important limitations. If you are on a first date and the other person asks you to pay, that might be perfectly fine. Or you may have a memory of how, every time a date asked you to pay, they never called again, leaving you thinking you'd been used for a free meal. You can suck it up and pay, then stew on it later, or you can shift, *drop to the blank screen*, and retrieve the memories of every time this has happened before—including how you planned to respond next time. With all that information literally at the top of your mind, you may decide to respond honestly and say, "That hasn't worked for me before." That would flip the responsibility back to the other person to make a decision for themselves based on the limit you're setting.

If the other individual has high self-esteem and acknowledges that you're using the way you've felt in the past to make a decision about paying, they might say, "Well, why don't we take turns paying for our dates?" You would pause, listen to yourself, and decide whether that's something you want to try. Even if it's not, at least you know they're listening to what you went through before and what's important to you.

This works with much more than money, as we've already seen. The fellow who's pushing by saying, "I want to do this" and "I want to do that" is triggering his date. She *drops to the blank screen* and responds honestly: "I hear what you're saying, but that doesn't work for me. It hasn't worked out well before."

The fellow with low self-esteem would think, *Ah, I'm not going out with her. She's too difficult.*

The fellow with high self-esteem would say, "Well, I hear you. And why don't we try this? A compromise."

When Relationships End: Dropping from a Breakup

Dropping isn't just effective in those very early interactions. It's a powerful tool in any phase of a relationship—even when the end is bitter. After all, one of the major experiences of dating is mourning the loss of a relationship. I see young people go through this all the time when they're dumped: mourning the loss of someone they are interested in who breaks up with them. Whether it's that someone doesn't ask for a second or third date, or the breakup comes after someone you've dated for years decides to move on, the resulting feelings are very close to mourning a loss.

Just like with mourning a loss, you're going to go through several stages of feelings—the well-known five stages of grief.

1. Denial, shock, and disbelief
2. Bartering
3. Sadness
4. Anger
5. Resolution or acceptance

The thing you need to know about mourning a loss is that the brain is very helpful in that process.

When you first experience a loss, your brain is going to flood you with thoughts and memories of that individual. Seems like torture, right? Actually, what the brain is doing is encouraging you to feel through your pain. As you've seen throughout this book, when you really feel through something—when you notice where you're lighting up, *drop to the blank screen* and allow yourself to experience and respond to personal memories and perspectives—that's when you can truly resolve those feelings. So, shortly after the loss happens, the brain is trying to help. It's trying to get you to go through those feelings in order to resolve them, so the memories of the loss come up less and less. The brain is assisting you in going through the very states of feelings needed to reach resolution.

When Relationships Last: Dropping in Marriage

Dropping to the blank screen is also very effective in marriage, which involves two people with two different upbringings coming together. You are likely used to doing different things or doing things two different ways. When you disagree, it can be easy to let those triggered feelings take over, resulting in impulsive reactions that are likelier to turn a minor conflict into an all-out fight. But that's not the only option.

If you understand how your spouse learned to deal with things growing up and how you learned to deal with things growing up, then you can each understand where the other's triggered feelings are coming from. If you have a conflict or a difference, instead of reacting, you can *drop to the blank screen*, retrieve experiences of similar disagreements, and determine your response based on what your brain reveals to you as the underlying tension or source of conflict. Then, you can gently call each other out on it. "Oh, you're acting like your mom again," or "Are you feeling this way because of how your dad used to treat you and your sister?" Once you've called out the source of your partner's behavior (or vice versa), you can diffuse the argument and work together toward a solution.

This method is helpful because we cannot expect people to be us. We have to get to know the people we are with and learn how they're wired. After that, we'll have the insight we need to *drop to the blank screen* and move forward respectfully and collaboratively when things aren't working very well.

Dropping into Your Ideal Dating Life

In your romantic relationships—as in all of the relationships we've explored in this book—you want to be seen as having high self-esteem and being respected. None of us want other people believing they can fill us with their disruption, their feelings, and their responsibilities.

The individual with high self-esteem is listening to and expressing their point of view. They know themselves and can be honest, and you walk away from an interaction with them filled with wonderful (and/or sexual) feelings that they have transferred to you. After all, life is about connecting with people. If you are with someone and you walk away feeling respected, you've had a good interaction. You're thinking about them in a pleasant way afterward, and you are left feeling calm. *That was fun*, you might think. *It was easy to connect with that person.*

Sounds fabulous, right? Practicing *dropping to the blank* screen will help you develop the high self-esteem you need to attract the kind of people who will enable you to create positive memories.

Chapter 10
Emotional Muscle: How Athletes and Performers Succeed

The mental approach of *dropping to the blank screen* can help athletes (and other performers) avoid being distracted as a tool to enhance performance and response. Cognitive distractions like memories of losing to a particular team or walking into an arena where they've performed poorly before can trigger anxiety, causing amateur and professional athletes to lose focus. Instead of performing optimally, a distracted athlete will be up in their head worrying about what happened last time and whether there will be a repeat.

You already know that these worries and triggered feelings come with simultaneous physical reactions. For athletes especially, these physical responses add an extra layer of complication. If their thoughts and worries continue, these will ultimately affect oxygen and blood flow to the brain, impacting the automatic and unconscious ability to follow through with what their bodies are trained to do in performance.

Another challenge for athletes is the temptation to get up in their minds before an event and paint pictures of the anticipated outcome. The pictures could be positive (*I'm going to go in and win this game, no problem*) or negative (*Gosh, is the same thing going to happen that happened last time?*).

Either way, they are a distraction that take you up into your head and impede you from being *dropped to the blank screen* such that your brain does not get enough oxygen to automatically and unconsciously execute the skills needed to perform well.

What's more, this visualization habit creates a full set of expectations that you really have no control over. Once the competition begins and one variable changes from what was previously envisioned—the other team scores when you didn't expect them to, for example—that triggers disappointment. Whether you're a professional swimmer at a meet or are playing at an informal pickleball tournament, you'll be thinking about that disappointment and what had been expected as opposed to *dropping* into a position where your athletic ability is automatically and unconsciously retrieved.

Thoughts aren't the only things to disturb athletes' execution of their skills. Fans, whether they're cheering or heckling, can cause a distraction. So can the other team's players, who may intimidate through actions or words. This can be intentional, such as trash-talking ("You're not really good as an athlete. Our team can beat you, no problem"), or unintentional, such as post-goal celebrations or their physical size and build.

Regardless of the source of the distraction, if you are up in your head, making predictions or worrying about what's going to happen, you aren't retrieving information from your brain about how to work with your body to achieve optimum performance as you respond to the ball or puck or opponent in front of you.

Dropping into the Competition

The mind plays a substantial role in the neuromuscular reactions and corresponding physiological responses we have to our emotions. In other words, we cannot think and feel without those thoughts and feelings triggering skeletomuscular responses. But here's the good news: just as in every other type of interaction, we can manage those tensions before and during a competition to restore the body to a more balanced state. Once there, we can make decisions based on realistic assessments of the situation on the field (or other athletic arena) in front of us rather than making assessments that are clouded by anticipation or worry.

The methodology for managing those tensions is, of course, *dropping to the blank screen*. Once you've mastered this strategy on the field, you'll find yourself able to remain in that critical state where your brain receives maximum oxygen and blood flow. The memory retrieval that occurs when you *drop to the blank screen* allows you to automatically retrieve everything your brain and body have already learned to do to perform in the expert way you've been trained.

When you're new to *dropping to the blank screen* as an athlete, it's important to recognize that you may have built up several competitions' (or even seasons') worth of unresolved emotions. This means that, when similar feelings are triggered, all those emotions will jump on board, too, making the new feeling enormous to *drop* through. So you may

> You may have to drop several times to get through those old feeling memories to a place where your body will be ready to perform

require more than just one *drop* to get to the *blank screen*. In fact, you may have to *drop* several times to get through those old feeling memories to a place where your body will be ready to perform.

Dropping on Ice: An MVP Perspective

I spoke with Jacob about his experience with distractions and *dropping to the blank screen* as an athlete. Jacob is a professional hockey player who's a pro at staying in neutral when things heat up on the ice. Jacob started with junior hockey, then D1 and D3 college athletics. In his senior year, he was awarded Defensive Player of the Year and Goaltender of the Year. Following this season, he was drafted to play professionally, and has continued to do so since college graduation.

Dr. Helen McKibben:

What is your thought process when an opposing player tries to provoke you while you're in the net?

Jacob:

My thought process is typically restrained. I don't really listen to what they say. I don't really think about what they meant. Instead, I try to tap into the emotion of what they said, and typically it's just anger or hurt. They're lashing out. I think when you can relate things, especially obstacles that are in your way, to basic childhood emotions, it really minimizes the threat in front of you. It just becomes a feeling you've seen before, and not really a threat. Because what is the opponent actually going to do to you? Nothing.

Dr. Helen McKibben:

If you are putting yourself in the position of the other player who's trying to provoke you, what do you think's going on?

Jacob:

When somebody is trying to irritate or distract you, they're trying to get you to think about their own agenda instead of your own ideas. Their sole goal is to disrupt your thought process and get you thinking about anything other than your specific positions and goals and what you came out to do today. You really have the option of tapping into how *you're* feeling or letting *their* emotions overtake you and disrupt your play.

Dr. Helen McKibben:

If someone can get you thinking about them instead of *dropping to the blank screen* where you'll retrieve memories of how to respond to that puck, it distracts you from performing the skill your brain already knows how to do.

Jacob:

Exactly. Whenever an opponent is trying to distract you, whether that's verbally, physically, or anything, they're trying to add to what you are thinking about. An athlete's already having to focus on a lot while they're engaged in the play, and the more you have to think about, the greater chance you have to make an error. Your opponents know that, and that's why they're trying to add another element to the physical and technical aspects you're already tracking.

Many sports professionals will tell you once the physicality becomes pretty much equal between two players or teams, 90 percent of winning or losing is about your emotional muscle and how you respond to what's currently in front of you without worrying about another person getting in the way. In sports, when milliseconds matter, your reaction time is everything. The more you have to deal with and think about, the slower you'll be to trust your automatic processes and make the right move for the situation.

It gives you a unique edge and dynamic advantage when you can change what your opponent is thinking.

> And it's equally important to put yourself in a position where your opponents *can't* do the same thing to you. Sports is all reacting.

Jacob is absolutely right: sports is all about reacting. The question is whether, when you're in a competition, you're reacting to the distractions around you (and the distractions in your head), or whether you're *dropping to the blank screen* to allow yourself to react only to the situation in front of you.

When to Drop for Optimal Performance

So given the variety of distractions in athletics, when do you drop?

In the last chapter, we briefly compared the timing of *dropping* to overcoming the fear of flying. Let's take a closer look at that analogy now. You can't resolve a fear of flying if you put off *dropping to the blank screen* until the first turbulence hits. Instead, you manage that fear by *dropping* every time you think about or take action toward flying on an airplane. You *drop* when you're buying the ticket. You *drop* the night before the flight. You *drop* while driving to the airport, while going through security, and again when you board the plane. You *drop* while you're buckling up your seat belt and again when you're taking off.

In other words, you *drop* every time you have feelings of anxiety. And how do you know you're feeling anxious? Because your brain will be lighting you up physically in the areas where you respond when you're triggered to feel. That is your cue to *drop to the blank screen*. And when you've done it every time you've sensed feelings of anxiety, you've resolved those feelings as they've come. Then, when the turbulence hits in-flight, the anxiety you have to *drop* through is minimal.

So, when do you *drop* in athletics?

The premise is the same. You *drop* every time you even think about playing the game. You *drop* every time you have a memory of playing that team before. You *drop* every time you have a memory of how the referee was unfair last time you played. You *drop* when you check your equipment. You *drop* while you're driving to the game, and when you hear people saying, "You're going to lose," or "You're going to win." You *drop* in the locker room as you're putting on gear. You *drop* while skating onto the ice rink. You *drop* during warm-ups.

This way, when something unexpected happens—when the other team scores, when there's gamesmanship occurring, when people are chiding or heckling you, or even when fans are cheering—you will only have to *drop* a minimal amount because you will have already resolved so many of your feelings, and you'll already be at a place where the *drop* to maximum performance is very brief.

To illustrate, Jacob shared with me his process of *dropping to the blank screen* before a big game.

Dr. Helen McKibben:

Tell me about your thought process going into a game.

Jacob:

For me, the lead-up to a game always started with the car ride to the rink. I would immediately start looking for things that felt familiar, like a song or a particular place I passed on the way to the rink. You play on the same arena most of your career, and you remember certain memories, whether they're positive or negative, that can prime you to start feeling a certain way.

I think it's very important to trust your *blank screen* and find that as often as you need. Whether your excitement gets too high and you start to feel too full of yourself or your associations are negative and you start to go to a place of no confidence, those memories and feelings can impact you more than you realize, unless you're conscious of them.

I can't control where I'm playing or how the game goes, but I can control whether I recognize my emotions going into it and try to get myself in the best headspace for me. I've had tremendous games where everything went right and it felt like I couldn't make a mistake, but I've also had games where absolutely everything went wrong. Instead of worrying about those bad days and trying to replicate the great ones or obsessing about how to be perfect, I realized that I'm better off starting in a baseline, or medium, physiological state. That's the best thought process I can get into going to a game—that neutral *blank screen*.

Dr. Helen McKibben:

When do you *drop to the blank screen*?

Jacob:

I feel like the best clue for what I need to *drop* is when my breathing starts to become irregular. If I start noticing my breathing, that helps me notice the other physiological responses that are going to hinder my ability to reach the *blank screen*.

Dr. Helen McKibben:

Sometimes anxiety comes from thinking about examples or memories ahead of time. One of the concepts we deal with in *dropping to the blank screen* is that, if something happens repetitively—if you have recurring anxiety about a game or a particular play or moment in a game—you have to have a method to resolve the anxiety every time it happens, not just when you're in the net.

Have you ever had to *drop* every time you even thought about the game in order to lower your level of anxiety so your brain could respond effectively to what was happening on the ice?

Jacob:

Yeah, absolutely. When I look back on playing, I think that there were four points prior to any game where the anxiety and physiological response built up enough for me to need to *drop*. Those points were the night before the game, waking the morning of, prior to going to the rink, and then prior to going on the ice. And I think the culmination of those four points—and the *drops*—is really what let me be calm when the moment finally came.

Before the game, like during those four moments, it's easy to find space and time to reach the *blank screen*, but in the actual competition, it's much harder. You have to find your spots, and you have to play between the whistles.

Nothing that matters or happens after the game play begins can get to you. There are only a few times where you get to take a step back, you get to take a moment away from what you're doing. If you spend those times focusing on what went wrong, you're going to repeat the same mistakes. Instead of focusing on what you did wrong, you just need to focus on nothing. And that's the hardest thing to do. Without the repetition of *dropping* beforehand, it's almost impossible. You need to prime yourself and practice the skill so it becomes an automatic response when you do feel that physiological response in your chest, or wherever you're holding it.

Dropping beyond Neutral

Dropping to the blank screen isn't simply about relieving neuromuscular tension, though that's certainly critical. As we've discussed, *dropping to the blank screen* resolves those physiological triggers so you get maximum oxygen and blood flow to the brain. But additionally, the method opens the door to memory retrieval of what's happened in similar situations so your brain can cue your body to respond to that game in the way you've been athletically trained to do.

So Step 1 may be something like "My nervous system went back to normal because I *dropped to the blank screen* and relaxed," but Step 2 is equally important: "I resolved that physiological reaction and got oxygen and blood flow to my brain, which allowed my brain to retrieve everything it knows about training to respond to the puck and the way it's coming at me."

Say, for example, that you're goalkeeping and the other team's star offensive player—who, by the way, is 6-foot-4 and lightning fast—is coming at you fast and hard with the puck. He's known for his trick shots, and you're nervous he'll get one by you. A quick *drop* will automatically help your brain recall what it's been trained to do: getting your anxiety out of the way and priming your body to stop this shot instead of thinking about your opponent.

Dropping to the blank screen is the quickest method to identify, go through, and resolve a triggered feeling so your brain and body can get back to top performance right away.

> *Dropping to the blank screen* is the quickest method to identify, go through, and resolve a triggered feeling so your brain and body can get back to top performance right away

To bring the idea to life, Jacob shares more about his experience maintaining a performance mindset during some of the most challenging parts of his athletic career.

Dr. Helen McKibben:

Have you ever had any experience where other players were trying to dismiss or minimize your experience during tryouts?

Jacob:

One of the things that comes out most in tryouts is feeling different. When you're playing with a group of people who objectively belong to that team and you're trying to make a place for yourself, it's easy to feel like an outsider. Maybe that's because of where you're from, your experience, the teams you've played on in the past, or your socioeconomic background. Whatever the reasons, feeling "other" can definitely cause anxiety during a time when athletes really need to be at their best. When you can learn to *drop to the blank screen* and play from a neutral mental state, it's much easier to stay focused on what really matters: your skills on the ice.

Dr. Helen McKibben:

Have you ever had coaches fail to follow through on what they said they would do for you?

Jacob:

Coming into any season, there's a lot of ambiguity about what roles different people will play. Whether you're very advanced in sports or a youth athlete, there's often a perspective that a coach has enticed them with a starting role or star position, and then when it comes down to it, that wasn't quite the reality. It can be pretty frustrating for players—especially youth players and their parents—and everybody associated with the organization.

Dr. Helen McKibben:

Have you ever had the experience of having to deal with heightened emotions after coaches did not follow through with what they promised you in tryouts?

Jacob:

Tryouts are obviously a time of great uncertainty, great potential prosperity, and good things to come. After that, I've definitely dealt with not only physical rage and being very upset, but also depression, feeling like you failed, and that there might not be hope.

What Jacob is describing here is an example of being set up to paint pictures based on what someone else says. A coach suggests that something may happen, and then when they don't follow through, players end up filled with disruption—feeling anger and rage that was not there before. The remedy for this is to be sure that when you find yourself up in your head painting pictures based on what someone else says, you shift and *drop* instead to hear your words and perspective to make a decision based on reality.

Dr. Helen McKibben:

In sports you learn what you're in control of and what you're not. As you went through junior and college and pro hockey, did that apply to you?

Jacob:

There were a lot of times when I felt completely hopeless because I was focusing on factors that I couldn't control, like statistics or the score of the game.

What I learned through the years was to focus not on the outcome but on my own process and my own reactions. There's always going to be a terrific player on the other team. There's always going to be a jeering fan.

But when you can go through the feelings those distractions bring—and then eventually block them out altogether—and focus on the things you can control and the things you enjoy about what you do, it really empowers you to let go of the things you can't control and ultimately find success based on your own feelings and decisions.

Dr. Helen McKibben:

How did you learn to shift back to yourself and make decisions about what was important to you?

Jacob:

It took a lot of trial and error, from early tryouts to just my career in athletics. But what I ultimately found is that I got in trouble when, right before the key moment, right before the physiological response built up, I wasn't focused on myself. The problems happened when I was focused on every other thing in the room, in the arena, on the ride there, every other factor.

Once I learned to *drop*, I realized it doesn't matter who's in the building or what else is going on, it only matters that I go out there and do what I love to do.

Dr. Helen McKibben:

When you faced distractions as an athlete—fans riding you from the stands, individuals trying to knock you off balance in the goal, walking into an arena where maybe you had lost games before—how did you transition from being triggered to focusing on the game?

Jacob:

It comes back to the *drop* technique and listening to myself and the actions I knew would lead me to success, and not to what I was provoked to do. Finding your own way to *drop*, no matter what you're doing— driving, walking, sitting in a crowded room or sitting alone, or even on the athletic field between whistles—is critical. When I learned to *drop*, I found a focal point that was always consistent and always reliable: myself.

I focused on myself and my feelings for success instead of relying on indicators of the past around me, like *I'm in this building* or *We're playing this team*. My focus was really only *I'm here. That's all I need for success*.

Dr. Helen McKibben:

In life, I have learned that resilience and persistence are what empower us to work toward our goals, to not be knocked off balance or stop doing what's important to us. Do you relate to resilience and persistence being important?

Jacob:

I think those are probably two of the most important concepts of any peak performer, along with enthusiasm. If you are really looking for a way to sustain and persist through adversity, think of your long-term goal and your cumulative efforts to get there. If you stick to what you love and what you know, no matter how many failures you have, you're going to find success in it.

I fell down thousands of times when I was learning to skate. When you're a kid, that's very easy to overcome, but as you grow older, you're "supposed" to face fewer failures.

There are definitely times I wanted to stop, not because I didn't love it but because I wasn't getting the payout or the success I wanted. But once I realized I could outlast a lot of the competition through enthusiasm, it really gave me motivation to be resilient and persistent in continuing my pursuit.

Building Emotional Muscle in Other Disciplines

Developing your emotional muscle is also relevant to musicians, writers, actors, and any other performer. And, just like in athletics, the distractions that compromise someone's emotional muscle can be external or internal. Externally, some instructors (like music teachers, theater directors, and writing coaches) can be cruel, creating anxiety in their students. The teacher and their teaching method can fill students with disruption. So can internal distractions, like the critical voice that says, "You're not good enough," or "You'll never land this role," or "Who would buy your book?"

When you feel anxiety or any other feeling, whether triggered by an external voice or an internal critic, you will light up physically. Your job, then, is to shift, notice exactly what areas are lighting up, and *drop to the blank screen* until your brain configures the words or ideas that are needed to perform your task.

If you *drop to the blank screen*, you will silence your critical voice or avoid taking on that teacher's cruelty or unresolved emotions, and you will return to optimal functioning. *Dropping to the blank screen* helps retrieve what your brain knows how to do and helps you focus on the music—or the canvas or empty page—in front of you instead of what some other voice is saying to you.

Just as in Jacob's hockey tryouts, *dropping to the blank screen* can be used when musicians, singers, or actors are going to auditions. When you're trying out for an orchestra, a musical group, or a play, you can use the same premise of overcoming the fear of flying to overcome anxiety.

Every time you even think about getting on the stage and trying out, every time you're practicing your audition piece, and every time you get into the car to drive to an audition, you can *drop to the blank screen*. As you're putting together your instrument or warming up, you can *drop to the blank screen*. If you've done this enough times throughout the preparation process, then by the time you are in the performance you'll already be at the *blank screen*. Rather than focusing on your nerves, your brain will be retrieving knowledge of how you were trained to perform. And if you do miss a note or make a mistake, you won't have to *drop* far to regain your composure and move forward with confidence.

Over the years of working with musicians, I've learned that some of their primary causes of anxiety are outside of their control, such as hearing whispers from other people or negative comments about other players in the orchestra. The politics of being selected triggers anxiety during auditions, and thinking about other people's perspectives can trigger anxiety even after you're cast or chosen. But whether you're in an audition or a performance, learning what you are in control of—your instrument and your thoughts alone—can be incredibly helpful. If you learn to *drop to the blank screen* and focus only on what you're in control of, your brain will retrieve and implement the only information that matters—your ability to perform.

Relying on your emotional muscle is also extremely important to actors who have to retrieve their memorized lines during each performance. If actors are up in their heads instead, worrying about remembering their lines, the neuromuscular reactions that go with that worry will build, decreasing blood and oxygen to the brain and inhibiting memory retrieval. In other words, worrying about remembering your lines makes it harder to remember your lines. But if an actor notices they're triggered, *drops to the blank screen*, and gets oxygen flow back to the brain, the brain will kick in and automatically and unconsciously retrieve lines from memory.

For an off-stage example, consider the last time you were in a hurry and couldn't find your keys. Were you running around the house, worrying about being late as you tried to find them? If so, your anxiety almost certainly caused a decreased oxygen flow to the brain. But the minute you stopped, *dropped*, and resolved that anxiety, you freed up your brain to recall where you left those keys.

Writers use emotional muscle, too, *dropping to the blank screen* to get the best words for their written material. Many of you do your best thinking at night because you have increased oxygen flow, which allows the brain to put together all your thoughts and memories and spit out words and ideas. This is best illustrated through those "lightbulb moments" that have you waking up in the middle of the night, saying, "Ah, that's what I'll do" or "That's what I'll say." The same is true for writers, but they often make their own "lightbulb moments" by putting themselves in situations where they are isolated from any distractions—and by *dropping to the blank screen* to get there—so they can access the words the brain is putting together for readers.

As these varied examples illustrate, any kind of performer will likely face distractions and triggered feelings throughout every step of their career. When facing these obstacles, you can reduce your anxiety and depression by *dropping to the blank screen*, which keeps emotions manageable and prevents you from being overwhelmed by predictive or negative thoughts, disruptions, and anxieties. This strategy enhances mental and physical performance by enabling you to focus on the task at hand: using your well-earned skills to wow your audience.

Chapter 11
Trusting Your Brain: It's Scientific

Now that you've read about how *dropping to the blank screen* can silence the critical voice, eliminate distractions, and enhance self-esteem in every area of your life, let's cover the details of how this methodology works and its importance in empowering you to achieve personal and professional goals.

Dropping to the blank screen works by freeing the brain to function in the way it is already designed to work for you. What makes *dropping* unique and different from other methods is that, rather than teaching you how to shut down or avoid emotions, it uses memory retrieval and decision-making to process those emotions and convert them into responses based on high self-esteem and the ability to live a life free from persistent thoughts and stressors.

Dropping to Manage Emotions

Emotion is an important topic in psychology and neuroscience, and it involves both physiological responses and emotional reactions. The autonomic part of the nervous system acts as a catalyst for physical responses in the retrieval of decision-making information from the brain, and triggered emotions are physical and psychological indicators of feelings present not only in the body, but also in thought processes.

If you don't have a method to detect and address triggered emotions, they will build up internally. This causes low self-esteem and makes it difficult to undertake sustainable, authentic, and confident decisions based on your own needs, perspectives, and desires. These feelings and their corresponding unconscious memories are often conveyed physically, so the quickest way to identify triggered feelings is through identifying your autonomic nervous system reactions. When you notice where you're "lighting up" physically, you can stop and identify what those reactions mean.

Dropping to Access Memories

Memory, like emotion, is critical in making decisions. Memories are sorted into subject matter categories by a part of the brain called the hypothalamus; the brain's amygdala retrieves those memories when relevant feelings are triggered in you. For example, when you get into a disagreement with a colleague, the amygdala will retrieve memories of difficult interactions with the same colleague, as well as similar disagreements with others. As a result, your thought processes are dependent on many levels of brain cell (neural) activity, some conscious and some unconscious. Thoughts are also influenced by the neural system's ability to imprint emotional experiences from childhood to adulthood, building new configurations in the brain that integrate past and present experiences. This enables you to have high self-esteem by stimulating the middle regions of the prefrontal cortex.

However, the brain mechanism for drawing on conscious and unconscious memory can run into problems if emotions aren't fully resolved. Those repressed emotions inhibit memory retrieval, leading the brain to focus instead on harmful distractions while corresponding physiological reactions—such as increased heart rate, blood pressure, and muscular contractions—continue to build.

The brain's limbic system, which is connected to neural pathways, may be thrown into imbalance when there are too many feelings to process at once. This causes emotions to shut down so they don't overwhelm your ability to function. Your body might shut down those emotions, but they will become automatic and unconscious. You never fully resolve them unless you *drop to the blank screen* and allow your limbic system to process one triggered feeling at a time.

In this way, emotion and memory work collectively to produce and enhance our decisions, which is why, in many cases, health care professionals must work both as psychotherapists and neuroscientists.

> Emotion and memory work collectively to produce and enhance our decisions

Dropping versus Other Therapies

When it comes to managing emotions, there are two common approaches or schools of thought. The first is mindfulness, which includes the arts of relaxation, letting thoughts go, and meditation. These are all physical techniques that resolve the physiology of triggered feelings. The second school of thought is analyzing or figuring out *why* you feel the way you feel in order to change *how* you feel. In my mind, those schools of thought can be helpful, but they do not go far enough because they don't resolve the actual feeling states that the individual is dealing with.

At one extreme of these methods, self-help books guide readers to cognitively control thought patterns. The other extreme is to simply use relaxation to release autonomic nervous system responses. Both of these methods place you at risk of diverting attention from the very feelings and corresponding words that you need to make good decisions.

The take-home is that no current therapies exist that fully integrate the link between emotions, physiology, and cognitive decision-making to resolve feelings. To truly support their clients, therapists must rethink therapy, incorporating the brain's emotional as well as cognitive functions.

Some therapy techniques support the fact that emotions can have physiological aspects, but the idea of changing the way we manage feelings by implementing or relearning this knowledge (or rewiring neural pathways) is underutilized. On the other hand, the *dropping to the blank screen* methodology described here leverages this knowledge to address both conscious and unconscious emotions and reverse their buildup in the brain and the body.

My technique of *dropping to the blank screen* monitors neuromuscular signals that indicate unconscious triggered emotions, past and present. The end result is integrating multiple levels of memory recall for making new decisions. Once those new decisions are enacted, individuals frequently share that the underlying emotions and corresponding physiological reactions are completely resolved. No other methods incorporate memory retrieval and the final, most important step of making decisions, which resolves emotions and prevents the recurrence of triggering thoughts or unhealthy actions.

This method is not simply reducing stress through relaxation, breathing, or mindfulness. It is a scientific, proven method to completely resolve feelings that could otherwise trigger you as a result of daily interactions with people, situations, or from thinking about people in past or present situations. The end result is peace of mind. No more spinning in your head, being flooded by the day's thoughts at bedtime, or by thoughts from the past.

Minimizing the Physical Impact of Stress

Stress is the physiological manifestation of unresolved feelings. When we are triggered to feel, if we don't have a method to completely resolve that triggered feeling, it keeps coming up over and over again, resulting in a physical reaction that builds with every recurrence of the negative feeling or thought. As the stress builds, that neuromuscular reaction starts squeezing off oxygen and blood flow to the brain.

Why is this important? Oxygen is the fuel brain cells use. The brain needs maximum oxygen flow to do what it is designed to do, which is to configure memory and your experiences into good decision-making. If you can't resolve triggered feelings and bring oxygen flow back up, feelings will keep building up, emotionally and physically, until you implode into depression or explode into anxiety and panic.

How do we reverse this buildup?

Think back to the fourth homework assignment I gave you in Chapter 1, to notice where you are lighting up physically when you are triggered to feel. If you have learned to become aware of when you are listening to the internal critical voice or when you're being disrupted by an external distraction, the first indicator will be that you're lighting up physically. Shifting to notice exactly where you're lighting up stops you completely from listening to that distraction. *Dropping to the blank screen* allows you to listen to your own words or ideas instead.

Whether you're running from feelings or facing disruption from other people, identifying where you light up physically is the first step in the methodology of going through how you feel and using that information to make decisions. Without taking these steps, the brain can't fully resolve feelings, and we'll keep thinking about it over and over again.

Dropping for High Self-Esteem

When you learn to *drop to the blank screen* and resolve the physiology of triggered feelings and the underlying emotions by making a decision based on your own feelings, experiences, and needs, you end up presenting with high self-esteem. Remember from Chapter 2 that I define *self-esteem* as having the ability to notice and listen to your own thoughts, feelings, and ideas, and to make decisions when ready.

Most self-help literature suggests that self-esteem can be defined as simply liking yourself, and it attempts to use relaxation strategies or strictly cognitive techniques to get you there. My method, on the other hand, redefines the clichéd "I like myself" concept of self-esteem and offers a new method that leverages the individualized biomechanics of emotion to engender fruitful decision-making.

Putting It All Together

We've reviewed the various elements and benefits of *dropping*, so let's take a moment to put the process together.

First, if a feeling is triggered, it is reflected in the body. Shift and notice where the feeling is lighting you up physically. *Dropping to the blank screen* resolves the physiology of the triggered feeling within the autonomic nervous system by moderating the sympathetic nervous system (fight or flight response) and activating the parasympathetic nervous system (neuromuscular release). One of the functions of the autonomic nervous system is to regulate the balance between the sympathetic nervous system and parasympathetic nervous system.

Second, keep *dropping*. If you stick with the process long enough, the brain will retrieve every memory of every time you felt this way before, including what's worked for you and what hasn't, and it will spit out simple words or ideas about what you can do so you don't feel this way anymore.

Third, use this information to make a decision about how to respond, which completely resolves the feeling for the brain.

If you go through the process of *dropping to the blank screen*, you will get to the point where you make confident decisions based on your own perspectives rather than rash reactions to your disruptors. This way, your brain will fully resolve your triggered feelings, and you won't think about them over and over again. Why is that important? Because if you keep thinking about them, the physiology behind the related memories keeps building, creating fertile ground for the critical voice to jump on board and try to influence what you say or do.

Remember, as you go through this process, you're achieving three things:

1. Resolving the physiology of feelings. *Dropping* enables you to do this completely and quickly, because it's not about going up into your thought processes to talk yourself into breathing deeper or relaxing. Instead, *dropping* provides a purely physical method that activates the brain's process for good decision-making.

2. Resolving current and underlying emotions. *Dropping* enables you to do this by connecting with your memory so you can make a decision and then move on.
3. Presenting with high self-esteem. Again, high self-esteem is what happens when a child or an adult listens to their own thoughts, feelings, and ideas in order to make decisions for themselves when they're ready.

Dropping to the blank screen quiets the critical voice, stops the pattern of running from feelings, and prevents you from reacting to other people, thus changing their read of you. By achieving all of these things, *dropping to the blank screen* breaks the cycle of unresolved feelings so you can move on with your life.

> Dropping to the blank screen quiets the critical voice, stops the pattern of running from feelings, and prevents you from reacting to other people

Implementing Your Decisions

Let's talk about these decisions you make when you've *dropped*. Because, after all, making and implementing a decision are the final steps to resolving feelings. The act of noticing feelings is not enough. As you know, the *dropping to the blank screen* method teaches individuals to use the brain in a way it is already designed to work. It uses your past and present emotional experience to make good decisions for yourself in order to resolve unresolved emotions so you can get back to enjoying your life in the moment.

These decisions, however, must be based on the memories your brain retrieves—and the analysis it spits out—when you've *dropped*. If your decisions are the result of emotional reactions to feelings or disruptions, you're opening the door for your critical voice to keep replaying the situations and retriggering the feelings endlessly. But if you make decisions based on what you hear when you *drop to the blank screen*, the brain will assure that you respond in a way that resolves the emotions and will ensure you won't feel that way again.

That said, even when you *drop*, you might not always make the right decision on the first try, and that's okay. If you pick an idea your brain presents, and you try it out but don't feel comfortable with the result, just pause, *drop* again, listen to your brain's other suggestions, and try a different idea until you find one you're comfortable with. You cannot fail with this method, because you can continue to *drop* as long as you need to until you land on the response that resolves your feeling and reinforces your high self-esteem.

Trust Your Brain, Trust Yourself

Dropping to the blank screen puts you in a position of self-reliance. It allows you to identify your own triggered feelings and use your brain in the way it is designed in order to configure the best decisions you can make for yourself. With this method, you don't have to recall what someone else told you to say or do, or what a book said to say or do. The *drop* methodology is built right into your very being, giving you everything you need to listen to yourself instead of others as you move through life.

Trust your brain. That's what this is all about. Your brain is already equipped with everything you need to identify and make excellent decisions for yourself. That is self-reliance.

Acknowledgements

Many thanks to Noah Gall and Amber Yoder for making this book possible. Your help with developing and compiling the manuscript as well as producing, recording, and editing the audiobook was crucial to the success of the book.

Thank you to all of the interview subjects who agreed to appear in this book and for sharing your life experiences.

Thank you to Sarah Welch for your developmental editing and wonderful comments on the manuscript. Thank you to Barbra Rodriguez for copy editing the manuscript. Thank you to Jenny Meadows for proofreading the manuscript.

Thank you to Emily Mahon for the fantastic cover design. Thank you to Rebecca Brown at Design for Writers for the wonderful interior design and proofreading.

And an enormous thanks to Stephanie Barko for your guidance and support, and for overseeing book publicity.

About the Author

Dr. Helen McKibben's approach combines the study of the body, the brain, and the interaction between emotions and memory. She created the technique of *dropping to the blank screen* after noticing two significant recurring needs among her clients. The first was the need to learn how to manage triggered emotions, and the second was understanding the root causes of their feelings.

Dr. McKibben earned her doctorate in psychology from California Southern University. Her thirty-five years of clinical work includes licensure in seven states and the District of Columbia, where she has her private practice. She also has national certification by the National Board for Certified Counselors.

Dr. McKibben's publishing credits include a psychological study of the therapeutic use of movement for people with Parkinson's disease and an article on the effects of internal and external distractions on the outcome of youth sports. For other works, including her Feelings Management podcast, please visit her website:

www.HelenMcKibben.com

Made in the USA
Columbia, SC
24 November 2024